£4.35

BUNTY ANNUAL
— 1995 —

SPECIAL RECIPE!

MIX WELL AND READ!
It's Yummy!

Printed and Published by D. C. THOMSON & CO., LTD.,
185 Fleet Street, London EC4A 2HS. © D. C. THOMSON & CO., LTD., 1994.
ISBN 0-85116-576-1

The Four Marys

IT was the end of term at St Elmo's and some of the girls were already heading home for the Christmas break —

BYE! HAPPY CHRISTMAS!

HAVE A GREAT HOLIDAY, EVERYONE.

SEE YOU NEXT TERM.

The Four Marys, Cotter, Radleigh, Field and Simpson, were staying behind.

WE'LL BE OFF IN A FEW DAYS OURSELVES. I WAS A BIT WORRIED WHEN I REALISED I HAD TO STAY AT SCHOOL AN EXTRA FEW DAYS BECAUSE MUM AND DAD ARE STILL AWAY, BUT THERE'S A CROWD OF US.

MRS MITCHELL ALWAYS UNDERSTANDS WHEN THINGS HOLD PEOPLE UP, FIELDY. SOMETIMES IT CAN'T BE HELPED.

WELL, I THINK IT'S GREAT WE'LL GET TO SPEND MORE TIME WITH EACH OTHER.

ME TOO, SIMPY. I WONDER IF WE'LL GET A WHITE CHRISTMAS, THIS YEAR?

WE MIGHT, COTTY. COME AND LOOK.

BRILL! I LOVE THE SNOW.

OOH, YES. I'M FEELING REALLY CHRISTMASSY NOW.

6

After tea —

THERE'S NOTHING LIKE AN AFTERNOON IN THE SNOW TO GIVE YOU A GOOD APPETITE. I'VE EATEN LOADS.

WE NOTICED, COTTY. ANYWAY, WE CAN RELAX NOW. AS WE'VE NO PREP TO DO, WE CAN WATCH TELEVISION ALL EVENING IF WE WANT.

So, later —

SNOW'S FALLEN ALL OVER THE COUNTRY, AND A LOT OF ROADS ARE BOCKED.

AND THEY'RE FORECASTING MORE. LET'S SEE IF IT'S STILL SNOWING HERE.

WHAT IF OUR PARENTS CAN'T GET THROUGH, VERONICA? WE CAN'T STAY HERE. I SHALL OBJECT TO THE SCHOOL GOVERNORS.

DO THEY EXPECT THE SCHOOL GOVERNORS TO STOP IT SNOWING? HONESTLY, THAT PAIR ARE ALWAYS COMPLAINING.

ME, TOO, MABEL. IT'S UP TO THEM TO SEE THAT EVERYONE CAN REACH ST ELMO'S.

THEY'RE PAINS. WE'LL JUST HAVE TO MAKE THE BEST OF THINGS.

Later that night —

IT'S STILL COMING DOWN THICK AND FAST. I EXPECT THE SNOWPLOUGHS WILL BE OUT TOMORROW.

I JUST WANT TO GO TO SLEEP. MM, I LOVE BEING WARM AND COSY.

But, next morning —

BRR! IT'S FREEZING!

LOOK AT THE TIME. THE RISING BELL SHOULD HAVE GONE HALF AN HOUR AGO. WHY DIDN'T IT?

Soon —

THE LIGHT DOESN'T WORK.

AND THE RADIATOR'S COLD. THERE'S BEEN A POWER CUT. THAT'S WHY THERE WAS NO RISING BELL.

WELL, WE'VE ALL PILED ON EXTRA JUMPERS, SO WE OUGHT TO KEEP WARM.

COME ON. BREAKFAST. I'M STARVING.

GOOD MORNING, GIRLS. THERE'S NO ELECTRICITY, I'M AFRAID. I'M JUST GOING TO REPORT IT AND HAVE IT RESTORED.

But —

THE PHONE'S DEAD. THE HEAVY SNOWFALL MUST HAVE BROUGHT DOWN THE CABLES. IT LOOKS LIKE WE'RE CUT OFF.

OH, NO!

WE WANT A HOT DRINK. THIS WON'T DO, WILL IT, VERONICA?

FOR GOODNESS SAKE, STOP WHINING, YOU TWO. IT'S NOBODY'S FAULT.

HUH! JUST LISTEN TO HER, MABEL. IT'S ALL VERY WELL FOR COMMON SCHOLARSHIP GIRLS LIKE SIMPSON, BUT WE'RE USED TO BETTER STANDARDS.

IGNORE THEM, SIMPY.

GOOD MORNING, GIRLS. COOK'S NOT BEEN ABLE TO GET HERE THIS MORNING, AND NOR HAS THE MILKMAN. SO WE'VE ONLY A LITTLE MILK, AND I'M AFRAID THERE ISN'T MUCH BUTTER LEFT, EITHER. THE MILKMAN USUALLY BRINGS THAT FOR US, TOO.

OH, NO! I SUPPOSE ALL THE MAIN SUPPLIES WERE USED UP BEFORE THE END OF TERM.

A few minutes later —

GENTLY NOW. RIGHT, LET'S TIE HER ON WITH SCARVES.

OKAY, SIMPY.

IT'S HARD GOING UPHILL LIKE THIS, COTTY.

YES, BUT WE'RE NEARLY THERE, FIELDY.

WE'LL SOON BE BACK AT SCHOOL NOW, ANDREA. JANE'S GONE ON AHEAD TO WARN THEM.

THANK YOU.

Back at St Elmo's —

CAN WE HAVE SOME BLANKETS? SHE NEEDS TO BE KEPT WARM.

AND SHE NEEDS TO GO TO HOSPITAL, BUT THE PHONES ARE STILL OUT OF ACTION.

I DON'T THINK AN AMBULANCE COULD GET THROUGH, ANYWAY. IF ONLY ST ELMO'S HAD ONE OF THOSE FOUR-WHEEL DRIVE VEHICLES, WE COULD TAKE HER OURSELVES.

AH! I'VE GOT AN IDEA.

A few minutes later —

I SAW THESE OLD SKIS THE OTHER DAY WHEN WE WERE EXPLORING THE ATTIC ROOMS. I CAN USE THEM. I'LL SKI FOR HELP.

BRILLIANT, RADDY. YOU'RE A GOOD SKIER.

I'M NOT SURE ABOUT THIS. IT'S SO DANGEROUS . . . OH, VERY WELL, IT'S OUR ONLY CHOICE. BUT DO BE CAREFUL

THERE SHE GOES. HURRY BACK, RADDY.

So —

The weather worsened as Raddy skied on —

ELMBURY AT LAST. THANK GOODNESS.

Two hours later —

RADDY'S BACK — WITH THE ARMY!

OF COURSE. ARMY AMBULANCES CAN USUALLY GET THROUGH WHATEVER THE WEATHER. THEY'RE SPECIAL VEHICLES.

YOU'VE DONE A GOOD JOB HERE. FIRST AID IS VERY IMPORTANT. YOU DID EXACTLY THE RIGHT THING FOR THE PATIENT.

THE SKIER DID WELL, TOO. YOU'D BETTER GO AND GET ALL YOUR BOXES, YOUNG LADY.

YOU'VE BROUGHT US FOOD SUPPLIES. BRILLIANT, RADDY.

ANDREA WILL BE OKAY. THEY'LL BE NEARLY AT THE HOSPITAL BY NOW. HEY, LOOK HERE — LOADS OF BASIC STUFF AND MINCE PIES AND CHOCOLATES. FANTASTIC!

OH, AND THE ELECTRICITY WILL PROBABLY BE BACK ON THIS AFTERNOON.

MINCE PIES

MILK CHOCOLATES

That afternoon —

IT'S LOVELY AND WARM NOW THE POWER'S BACK ON. AND THE SNOW'S STOPPED!

EVERYTHING'S ALMOST BACK TO NORMAL.

Soon —

THE PHONE'S WORKING AGAIN, AND I'VE CONTACTED THE HOSPITAL. ANDREA IS FINE. AND SHE'S GOING TO BE TRANSFERRED TO A HOSPITAL NEAR HER HOME. BUT THE OTHER NEWS IS THAT THE SNOWPLOUGHS WON'T BE HERE FOR A FEW DAYS.

SO WE'RE MAROONED?

Later —

WHO CARES ABOUT BEING MAROONED AT ST ELMO'S WHEN WE'RE ALL TOGETHER? I'M LOOKING FORWARD TO CAROLS ROUND THE TREE.

HEAR THAT, VERONICA? THOSE FOUR ARE SO CHEERFUL IT MAKES ME SICK.

On Christmas Eve —

HAPPY CHRISTMAS, YOU THREE. I THOUGHT YOU'D BE OPENING THESE AT HOME. WE DIDN'T EXPECT TO BE STILL HERE ON CHRISTMAS EVE, DID WE?

BUT IT'S GREAT TO BE TOGETHER. THAT MAKES IT A SPECIAL CHRISTMAS. HAPPY CHRISTMAS, EVERYONE!

THE END

Secret Schoolgirl

BRILLIANT GOAL! AMY'S WON THE MATCH FOR US!

SHE ALWAYS DOES! WE HAVEN'T LOST A GAME SINCE SHE'S BEEN CAPTAIN.

AMY HOWARD had only spent one term at Blackstone Academy, but already she had made her mark as one of the most popular and talented pupils at the school.

WELL DONE, AMY!

THANKS, NINA!

I THOUGHT I WOULDN'T SETTLE HERE AT BLACKSTONE, WHEN MUM AND DAD HAD TO GO ABROAD, BUT IT'S GREAT! EVERYTHING SEEMS TO BE GOING SO WELL FOR ME.

AMY! WILL YOU GO TO THE HEAD'S STUDY? SHE WANTS TO SPEAK TO YOU.

OH!

I WONDER WHAT MISS LENNOX WANTS ME FOR? I HOPE I'M NOT IN TROUBLE!

I'M AFRAID THERE IS VERY BAD NEWS FOR YOU, AMY. THE PLANE YOUR PARENTS WERE TRAVELLING IN HAS BEEN LOST IN THE AMAZON JUNGLE AND THERE SEEMS TO BE VERY LITTLE HOPE THAT ANYONE HAS SURVIVED.

OH, NO! THAT CAN'T BE TRUE! MUM AND DAD CAN'T BE DEAD!

THERE NOW, MY DEAR. IT'S A TERRIBLE SHOCK FOR YOU, BUT YOU MUST TRY TO BE BRAVE. IT'S BEEN ARRANGED THAT YOU ARE TO GO AND LIVE WITH YOUR AUNT IN LONDON. I KNOW I SPEAK FOR ALL THE STAFF WHEN I SAY WE SHALL BE MOST SORRY TO SEE YOU GO.

I CAN'T BEAR IT! NEVER TO SEE MUM AND DAD AGAIN AND TO LEAVE BLACKSTONE AS WELL. THINGS WOULDN'T HAVE BEEN QUITE AS BAD IF I COULD HAVE STAYED HERE WITH MY FRIENDS. BUT TO HAVE TO LEAVE SO SUDDENLY AND GO AND LIVE WITH SOMEONE I DON'T EVEN KNOW — IT'S HORRIBLE!

Next day —

WE'LL MISS YOU TERRIBLY, AMY. THINGS WON'T BE THE SAME WITHOUT YOU. PROMISE YOU'LL WRITE TO US!

OF COURSE I WILL.

LIZ, JANE AND NINA ARE THE BEST MATES ANYONE COULD HAVE. I'LL MISS THEM SO MUCH.

Later —

I'VE BEEN SO HAPPY HERE, BUT IT'S NO GOOD HOPING I MIGHT COME BACK — IT'S PROBABLY TOO EXPENSIVE FOR AUNTIE BETTY TO PAY FOR ME TO STAY.

When Amy arrived at her new home —

HELLO, AUNTIE BETTY! I'M AMY!

OH! IT'S YOU. I DIDN'T EXPECT YOU SO SOON. WELL — I SUPPOSE YOU'D BETTER COME IN.

YOU'LL SLEEP IN HERE. AND THERE'S TO BE NO RADIOS OR RECORDS — I'M NOT HAVING ANY OF THAT NOISY RUBBISH. GET YOUR THINGS UNPACKED AND COME DOWNSTAIRS — YOU CAN HELP ME MAKE THE DINNER.

WHAT A WELCOME! AUNTIE BETTY DOESN'T SEEM AT ALL PLEASED THAT I'M HERE.

YOU START AT HOLMEVIEW HIGH SCHOOL TOMORROW — THAT'S THE BIG COMPREHENSIVE DOWN THE ROAD. THERE'S A SECOND-HAND UNIFORM FOR YOU IN THE WARDROBE. I'M NOT SPENDING GOOD MONEY ON EXPENSIVE CLOTHES FOR YOU TO MESS UP.

I DON'T THINK I'M GOING TO LIKE IT HERE. BUT IF I TRY TO FIT IN, MAYBE AUNTIE BETTY WILL GET TO LIKE ME. THIS IS MY NEW HOME, SO I'LL HAVE TO MAKE THE BEST OF IT.

Next day, at Amy's new school —

HUH! SHE REALLY THINKS SHE'S SOMEONE SPECIAL, COMING FROM THAT POSH BOARDING SCHOOL. WE'LL SOON CUT HER DOWN TO SIZE!

IT'S *AWFUL* HERE! I'LL NEVER FIT IN. I'D GIVE ANYTHING TO BE BACK AT BLACKSTONE WITH JANE, NINA AND LIZ.

A few days later —

HURRY UP AND FINISH THAT WASHING-UP. I'VE GOT FRIENDS COMING ROUND TONIGHT AND I WANT YOU OUT OF THE WAY.

OH — I JUST HATE IT HERE! I'VE TRIED TO GET ON WITH AUNTIE BETTY, BUT SHE TREATS ME LIKE A SKIVVY. I'VE HAD ENOUGH!

Meanwhile, at Blackstone School —

ISN'T IT QUIET WITHOUT AMY? IT'S ODD THAT SHE'S NOT WRITTEN. I THOUGHT WE'D HAVE HAD A LETTER OR SOMETHING BY NOW TO SAY HOW SHE'S GETTING ON.

I HOPE SHE'S OKAY. I DON'T THINK SHE WAS REALLY LOOKING FORWARD TO LIVING WITH THAT AUNT OF HERS.

At midnight that night —

LIZ! NINA! WAKE UP! SOMEONE'S THROWING STONES AT THE WINDOW.

NINA! IT'S ME — AMY! WILL YOU LET ME IN?

AMY! YOU'RE SOAKED! OF COURSE YOU CAN COME IN. CLIMB UP — WE'LL GIVE YOU A HAND.

Soon —

IT WAS AWFUL WITH AUNTIE BETTY. I COULDN'T BEAR TO STAY THERE ANOTHER NIGHT. WILL YOU HIDE ME HERE FOR A LITTLE WHILE?

OF COURSE WE WILL, AMY. BUT WHAT ABOUT YOUR AUNT? WON'T SHE START LOOKING FOR YOU WHEN SHE FINDS YOU'VE GONE?

20

CONTINUED ON PAGE 71

ANNIE'S STORY

IT was April 1985 and ten-year-old Annie Freeman and her parents had just moved to the tiny village of Brockbridge, where Annie was enjoying her first Spring in the country.

Annie was soon on her way to school—

MORNING, LASS! LOOKS LIKE IT'LL BE A GRAND DAY.

THERE! I'VE JUST THE HENS TO FEED, AND THEN I'LL GET READY FOR SCHOOL.

YOU'RE A GOOD GIRL, ANNIE! BUT DON'T BE LATE — I KNOW HOW MUCH YOU LOVE YOUR LESSONS.

GOOD MORNING, MISTER JACK! IT'S LOVELY, ISN'T IT? I CAN'T WAIT TO SEE THE FLOWERS IN BLOOM.

ANNIE'S A GRAND LASS — ALWAYS READY WITH A SMILE, AND A FRIEND TO EVERYONE. YOU'D THINK SHE'D LIVED HERE ALL HER LIFE. WHAT BROUGHT HER FAMILY TO BROCKBRIDGE?

THERE'S THE SCHOOL BELL RINGING! I MUST HURRY. OH! POOR LITTLE DANNY'S FALLEN DOWN.

NO-ONE KNOWS. ALL I KNOW IS IT DOES YOU GOOD TO SEE THE LITTLE LASS AROUND — SO FULL OF LIFE AND LAUGHTER.

That's a nasty graze, Danny. Can you be brave and try to walk? Look — you can take this apple for your dinner.

Oh, thank you, Annie!

It was half *my* dinner, but I don't mind. Danny's family is so poor that he usually only has a crust.

In the tiny schoolroom —

Move over, Sam! I want to sit by Annie!

No! I'm staying here. You sat beside her yesterday.

Huh! Look at those stupid brats, Ellen! Fancy wanting to sit beside Miss Goody-Goody!

Later —

Well done, Annie! You're a model pupil. If only everyone would work as quickly as you. You can clean the blackboard now and help the little ones with their work.

Oh!

Careful, Annie! You might hurt yourself!

Ha! Ha! Serves her right! It isn't natural, loving school like she does!

I'm sure that wasn't an accident. I'd like to be friends with Mary and Ellen, but they don't like me. Maybe it's because I'm new here?

Later —

It will soon be May Day. Tomorrow we must choose our May Queen and practise the Maypole dance.

A May Queen! There was never anything like this in the town. What a wonderful way to welcome spring!

On the way home —

That's one of Farmer Grey's hens. She must have a nest in the hedge. I wonder if there are any eggs?

22

23

A DANCER'S DREAM

FOR as long as she could remember, Hannah Armitage's dream had been to be a ballerina.

JUST GO OVER THOSE STEPS AGAIN BEFORE YOU GO HOME, GIRLS.

OH, NO! THE LESSON CAN'T BE NEARLY OVER ALREADY? TIME JUST SEEMS TO FLY BY WHEN I'M DANCING.

I WISH I COULD DANCE EVERY DAY, INSTEAD OF JUST ONCE A WEEK! I'D GIVE ANYTHING TO GO TO A PROPER BALLET SCHOOL, BUT I KNOW MUM AND DAD COULDN'T POSSIBLY AFFORD IT.

HANNAH! I'D LIKE TO HAVE A WORD WITH YOU.

HOW WOULD YOU LIKE TO TRY FOR A SCHOLARSHIP AT THE ROSETTA DANCE ACADEMY? YOU'VE A LOT OF TALENT.

I'D LOVE TO. IT'S ONE OF THE TOP BALLET SCHOOLS. I'M SURE MUM AND DAD WILL LET ME TRY.

Two weeks later —

FANTASTIC! THE ROSETTA DANCE ACADEMY'S ACCEPTED ME FOR AN AUDITION. I'VE TO GO THERE FOR A WEEKEND NEXT MONTH.

Three weeks later, Hannah arrived at the Rosetta Dance Academy.

SO YOU'RE HANNAH ARMITAGE? YOU'LL BE SHARING A ROOM WITH TWO OTHER GIRLS IN THE WEST WING. I'LL SHOW YOU THE WAY.

THANK YOU.

THIS IS A BRILLIANT PLACE, BUT I MUSTN'T BUILD UP MY HOPES. THERE MUST BE LOTS OF GIRLS HERE FOR THE AUDITION WHO ARE JUST AS KEEN AS ME TO WIN IT.

HI! ARE YOU SHARING WITH US? I'M STEPHANIE COLLIER AND THIS IS NICOLA BARKER.

HELLO! I'M HANNAH. SO YOU'RE HERE FOR THE AUDITION TOO?

THAT'S RIGHT. DON'T BUILD UP YOUR HOPES. ONLY REALLY GOOD DANCERS LIKE ME WILL STAND A CHANCE.

OH!

WHAT A BIGHEAD! THAT'S PUT ME IN MY PLACE.

I'M GOING TO THE PRACTICE ROOM. WE CAN GO IN THERE WHENEVER WE LIKE.

GOOD IDEA! I'LL COME WITH YOU.

COUNT ME OUT. BUT DON'T LET ME STOP YOU, IF YOU NEED THE PRACTICE.

I'M SO NERVOUS! I'M SURE TO MAKE A MESS OF THE AUDITION.

DON'T WORRY! JUST DO YOUR BEST. AND DON'T LET NICOLA PUT YOU OFF. I DON'T SUPPOSE SHE'S ANY BETTER THAN WE ARE.

THE AUDITION WILL BE TOMORROW AFTERNOON, SO WE'VE SOME TIME TO SETTLE IN.

THERE ARE SIX GIRLS HERE FOR THE AUDITION. THEY ALL LOOK MUCH BETTER THAN ME. AT LEAST STEPHANIE AND THE OTHERS ARE FRIENDLY — NOT LIKE SNOOTY NICOLA.

Later —

AFTER YOUR MEAL, I'LL SHOW YOU ROUND THE SCHOOL. WE HAVE MANY SOUVENIRS FROM FORMER PUPILS WHO HAVE BECOME FAMOUS BALLERINAS.

BRILLIANT! THIS IS A FAB PLACE, ISN'T IT? I'D GIVE ANYTHING TO COME HERE!

ME TOO! THAT'S MADAME YVETTE, THE PRINCIPAL.

27

HUH! WHAT A DRAG. I'D RATHER SIT IN THE COMMON ROOM AND WATCH THE TELLY. BUT I SUPPOSE I'D BETTER GO ALONG WITH YOU.

TO THINK THAT ALL THESE GREAT BALLERINAS WERE HERE AS PUPILS! IT'S A *PRIVILEGE* TO BE ALLOWED TO AUDITION HERE.

NICOLA'S NOT REALLY INTERESTED AT ALL — SHE'S JUST TRYING TO MAKE A GOOD IMPRESSION.

Later —

MUM THOUGHT I MIGHT STARVE THIS WEEKEND, SO SHE PACKED UP ALL THESE GOODIES FOR ME! DIG IN — I DAREN'T TAKE ANYTHING HOME AGAIN!

YUMMY! THANKS, HANNAH!

YEAH! I'LL HAVE ONE.

NICOLA'S NOT TOO SNOOTY TO TRY OUT MUM'S BAKING! THERE'S PLENTY FOR EVERYONE AND MAYBE JOINING IN WILL MAKE HER MORE FRIENDLY.

But, at bedtime —

BREAKFAST IS AT EIGHT TOMORROW. MADAME YVETTE SAID SHE WANTED EVERYONE TO BE ON TIME, AS SHE'S TAKING A CLASS FOR US AT NINE.

RIGHT! I'LL SET MY ALARM FOR HALF-PAST SEVEN.

WHY — NICOLA'S CASE IS CRAMMED FULL OF CHOCOLATE AND CRISPS, AND SHE DIDN'T OFFER TO SHARE THEM WITH US.

I'M TOO EXCITED TO SLEEP, THINKING ABOUT THE AUDITION TOMORROW. I *MUST* DO WELL! I'LL NEVER HAVE ANOTHER CHANCE LIKE THIS.

Hannah finally drifted off to sleep. Next morning —

STEPHANIE! WAKE UP! IT'S NEARLY EIGHT O'CLOCK! WE MUST HAVE SLEPT THROUGH THE ALARM! NOW WE'LL BE LATE FOR BREAKFAST.

A few minutes later —

AH! AT LAST! YOU HAVE MISSED MY INSTRUCTIONS. SEE ME AFTER BREAKFAST.

MADAME YVETTE ISN'T TOO PLEASED THAT WE'RE LATE. BUT WHY DIDN'T THE ALARM GO OFF?

NICOLA WAS UP BEFORE US. WHY DIDN'T SHE WAKEN US? PERHAPS SHE *WANTED* US TO BE LATE, AND TURNED OFF MY ALARM? NO — SHE'S BIGHEADED AND SELFISH, BUT I'M SURE SHE WOULDN'T HAVE DONE A SPITEFUL THING LIKE THAT.

Later —

MADAME'S A FABULOUS TEACHER — IT WOULD BE ACE TO BE IN HER CLASS. BUT I DON'T THINK THERE'S MUCH CHANCE FOR ME. THE OTHERS ARE SO MUCH BETTER THAN ME.

After class —

HOW DID YOU GET TO BE AT THIS AUDITION? YOU'RE *RUBBISH!* AND WHAT A SCRUFFY OUTFIT! I'D BE ASHAMED TO BE SEEN IN THAT PATCHED LEOTARD. I'M SURPRISED MADAME YVETTE HASN'T SENT YOU HOME!

BUT — BUT — I HAVEN'T ANYTHING ELSE.

OH, NO! HOW COULD NICOLA BE SO CRUEL? GAIL TOLD US HER DAD'S OUT OF WORK AND SHE COULDN'T AFFORD A NEW LEOTARD. NOW SHE'S REALLY UPSET.

29

However, a few evenings later —

I WOULDN'T ADMIT IT TO MARTIN, BUT IT'S PRETTY EXCITING, NEVER KNOWING WHAT YOU'LL PICK UP ON HIS SATELLITE DISH!

ZANG ZERT POOT!

GOOD GRIEF, WHAT PROGRAMME IS THAT? I DON'T RECOGNISE THE LANGUAGE AT ALL!

THIS IS PLUTO TELE-CONTACT. I HAVE NOW ADJUSTED MY SPEECH TRANSLATOR. WE SHOULD HAVE NO MORE TROUBLE, CALLER.

MUST BE A DRAMA PROGRAMME. IT'S WEIRD THOUGH, ALMOST AS IF THAT GIRL WERE TALKING STRAIGHT TO ME.

OF COURSE I'M TALKING TO YOU, CALLER. I'M AURORA FROM ZONE 5. PLEASE IDENTIFY YOURSELF.

I — I'M KAREN KNIGHT AND THIS IS RODWAY ROAD, IN DIDWICH. BUT I DON'T UNDERSTAND HOW YOU CAN TALK TO ME THROUGH THIS TV!

HEY! I'VE BEEN TRYING FOR MONTHS TO GET INTO TELE-CONTACT WITH SOMEONE FROM ANOTHER PLANET. HAVE I ACTUALLY SUCCEEDED AT LAST? IS 'DIDWICH' A PLANET?

Just then —

MARTIN, I JUST MADE CONTACT WITH A GIRL ON ANOTHER PLANET, BUT THE PICTURE'S BROKEN UP! WE COULD EVEN SEE EACH OTHER!

HA! HA! VERY FUNNY. ONE DAY YOU'LL STOP TAKING THE MICKEY OUT OF MY SATELLITE DISH AND REALISE HOW BRILLIANT IT IS!

MAYBE I JUST IMAGINED THAT CONVERSATION — BUT IF I REALLY DID JUST TALK TO A GIRL FROM PLUTO, MARTIN'S DISH IS BETTER THAN EVEN *HE* COULD EVER HAVE REALISED.

The following evening —

IT'S AURORA AGAIN, KAREN! I HOPED THAT I WOULD FIND YOU AGAIN. PLEASE CONFIRM OR DENY THAT DIDWICH IS A NEW PLANET, AS YET UNKNOWN TO OUR SCIENTISTS ON PLUTO.

DIDWICH IS A LITTLE TOWN ON *EARTH* — BUT I'M BEGINNING TO SUSPECT THIS IS A TRICK! IT'S IMPOSSIBLE TO SEE EACH OTHER THROUGH THE TV!

WHAT IS THAT STRANGE DISC YOU ARE PUTTING IN YOUR MOUTH? IS IT EARTH FOOD?

YOU REALLY CAN SEE ME! TELL ME A BIT MORE ABOUT THIS TELE-CONTACT THING! I'D LIKE TO KNOW ABOUT YOU TOO.

I LIVE ON PLUTO, WITH MY PARENTS AND BROTHER. WILL YOU BE MY TELE-FRIEND? WE COULD SPEAK TO EACH OTHER EVERY DAY.

THAT'S A BIT LIKE A PEN PAL, I SUPPOSE. HEY, I CAN'T WAIT TO BRING MY BEST MATE SHEILA TO SEE YOU.

So, after school the next day —

YOU'LL REALLY LIKE AURORA. WE HAD A REALLY LONG CHAT YESTERDAY. SHE'S FIVE HUNDRED AND TEN IN PLUTO YEARS, WHICH MAKES HER ABOUT OUR AGE . . .

DON'T YOU THINK YOU'RE GETTING A BIT OLD FOR SILLY JOKES?

OH, NO! AURORA WARNED ME THAT IF THERE WERE ANY INTER-GALACTIC METEOR STORMS, WE COULD LOSE COMMUNICATION.

IF THE JOKE'S OVER, CAN I GO HOME? WE HAVE TO DO THAT GROTTY FRENCH ESSAY. YOU OUGHT TO GET ON WITH IT, INSTEAD OF PLAYING THE FOOL.

I CAN ONLY STAY FOR FIVE OF YOUR EARTH-HOURS BEFORE STARLAN BEAMS ME BACK ABOARD. I HOPE THAT WILL BE TIME FOR ME TO SEE YOUR SCHOOL.

I CAN'T WAIT TO INTRODUCE YOU TO SHEILA. SHE'LL HAVE TO BELIEVE ME NOW!

THIS IS AURORA, MY TELE-FRIEND FROM PLUTO.

AND I'M KYLIE MINOGUE! HONESTLY, KAREN, WHEN ARE YOU GOING TO STOP BEING SO CHILDISH!

OH, MISS DONNELLY, THIS IS MY — ER — PEN PAL, AURORA. SHE'S VISITING FOR THE DAY. SHE'S BORROWED MY SPARE UNIFORM.

SHE NEVER TOLD ME SHE HAD A PEN PAL!

YOU'RE WELCOME TO SIT IN ON MY CLASS, DEAR. ARE YOU FAMILIAR WITH ALGEBRA?

$\sqrt{36-32}$ over 2 $6x + 8 = 0$ $a = 4$ $b = 6, c = 8$

I SEE, THIS IS SOME FORM OF MATHEMATICAL WORK. PERSONALLY, I'VE JUST REACHED GRADE B OF ADVANCED MOLECULAR AND ANTI-GRAVITAL MULTI-DIVISION.

OH — ER — I SEE! YOU MUST BE DOING A DIFFERENT SYLLABUS IN YOUR SCHOOL.

I HOPE YOU'RE NOT BORED!

CERTAINLY NOT! IT'S FASCINATING TO SEE YOUR ANCIENT METHODS OF CALCULATION. ON PLUTO, WHAT YOU ARE DOING NOW COULD BE UNDERTAKEN BY THE YOUNGEST PUPILS.

At lunch-time, in the local café —

YOUR PEN PAL CERTAINLY HAS AN APPETITE, BUT WHY ARE YOU PAYING?

SHE DIDN'T BRING HER MONEY.

THIS WILL TAKE ALL MY ALLOWANCE FOR THE NEXT MONTH!

38

I'D BETTER GO HOME. AURORA'S TRANSLATOR WAS POINTING AT HER WHEN I TOUCHED IT, SO NOW I SPEAK AND UNDERSTAND HER LANGUAGE. I CAN'T SEE ANYONE BELIEVING THAT ONE!

For the next couple of days —

IF YOU DON'T GET BETTER TODAY, I'LL MAKE YOU AN APPOINTMENT AT THE SURGERY.

I LET MUM THINK I HAD A SORE THROAT, SO I DIDN'T HAVE TO SAY ANYTHING. I'VE TRIED TO CONTACT AURORA, BUT WITHOUT ANY LUCK! LET'S HOPE I MANAGE IT TODAY.

Later —

AURORA! BTZ DANG!

OH, POOR KAREN! I FEARED THIS MIGHT HAVE HAPPENED, BUT DURING MY JOURNEY BACK HOME, I HAD NO MEANS OF CONTACTING YOU. I'LL FETCH THE TRANSLATOR, TO PUT THINGS RIGHT.

Soon —

WE ARE LOSING TRANSMISSION AGAIN — MUST BE ANOTHER METEOR STORM.

IT'S ALL RIGHT! YOU'VE PUT ME BACK TO NORMAL AGAIN. I'LL TELL YOU WHAT HAPPENED AT SCHOOL, NEXT TIME WE'RE IN TELE-CONTACT.

But —

THE NEIGHBOURS COMPLAINED TO THE COUNCIL! THEY SAID I HAVE TO HAVE PLANNING PERMISSION TO ERECT ANOTHER ONE — BUT I SHAN'T BOTHER! IT'LL NEVER BE THE SAME.

MARTIN, WHY ARE YOU TAKING DOWN YOUR SATELLITE DISH?

MARTIN'S RIGHT. IT WAS A MILLION-TO-ONE CHANCE THAT HE GOT TUNED INTO PLUTO'S WAVELENGTH. I WONDER IF I'LL EVER HAVE ANOTHER CHANCE TO BE AURORA'S TELE-FRIEND?

THE END

COVER

Emma arrives at our photographer's studio with "clean" face and hair which means no make-up or hair products — but still manages to look lovely! Mum comes along, too, to keep her company.

Make-up artist, Gena, gets to work applying a very light, natural make-up so that Emma's face doesn't appear shiny under the studio lights. This consists of an even coat of foundation or tinted moisturiser applied to the face and neck with a cosmetic sponge . . .

. . . a light dusting of translucent powder to set the base . . .

With everyone standing by, Emma takes her place in front of the camera and our photographer, Darren, helps pose and position her.

First he takes a test shot called a Polaroid to get an idea of how the picture will eventually look. Here he is showing it to Emma.

Emma changes outfits and hairstyles and has her make-up touched up throughout the day. Heaps of photos are taken in different poses and expressions so we've got a big choice at the end of the day.

ALL

EMMA Griffiths-Malin is the gorgeous glamorous girlie who you can see on the cover of this Bunty Annual! Emma comes from London where she does modelling jobs through an agency called Little Boats. They have loads of other models on their books including girls like Emma, families, babies and boys, too! Clients look through the agency's book at all the models' photos and choose a model to suit their needs. We chose Emma because she's so fresh and lively!

EMMA started modelling two years ago when she was "discovered" by a friend's mum at a party. Since then she's been to Vienna to make a TV ad for Austrian coffee, modelled for Bunty (of course) and had loads of other jobs to keep her busy. Although this takes up most of her spare time, Emma reckons it's worthwhile. The cash she makes while modelling provides her with plenty of pocket money for a start! And although it's hard work, Emma thinks her modelling jobs are mostly great fun, too.

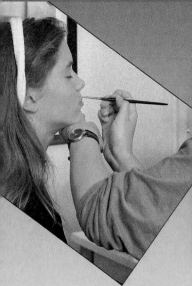

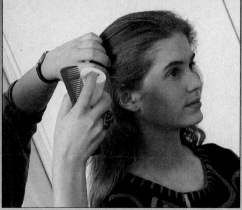

Gena is also a hairdresser and changes Emma's hair throughout the day.

A member of the Bunty staff chooses some outfits for Emma to wear during the photo session. The clothes and accessories are borrowed from a selection of High Street shops including Tammy Girl and C & A. They'll be returned afterwards.

and finally a coat of rosy lipstick applied with a brush, one coat of mascara on the top lashes y, and some very pale, browny eyeshadow on the elid! The over-all effect is that under studio lights d before the camera, Emma appears to be wearing no make-up at all!

Emma finds time for a quick bite to eat between photos!

And after a hard day's work it's time to say goodbye to the Bunty team and head for home.

Here's the finished product. Emma adorns the cover of this year's BUNTY ANNUAL.

ABOUT

EMMA admits to getting a bit embarrassed when friends at school see her in magazines and newspapers, but most of her friends are really used to it by now. Fashion-wise she's really into wearing black clothes at the mo' which has something to do with her obsession with The Rocky Horror Show — she's mad on it! Lucky Emma says she doesn't follow any special beauty routine to keep looking good — she just washes and conditions her hair and skin regularly. Sixties style songster, Lenny Kravitz, is her pop fave and she's into rock music generally.

EMMA would love to continue modelling when she gets older and go into acting, too! She's had a small part in the Rocky Horror Show already! If you think you've got what it takes to be a model, Emma advises you to get some nice, clear snapshots of yourself done and send them to a good, reputable agency with all your details, too. But remember to consult your mum and dad beforehand!

Latr Lisa

IT'S CHRISTMAS BUT YOU'D NEVER KNOW IT! I'M THE ONLY ONE WITH ANY FESTIVE CHEER!

See what I mean?

NO, ANDREW. ABSOLUTELY NOT.

BUT WE SHOULD HAVE A REAL CHRISTMAS TREE THIS YEAR, SUSAN. THEY LOOK SO MUCH BETTER.

EXCEPT THEY DROP NEEDLES ALL OVER THE PLACE. AND THEY SMELL.

43

44

WHERE ARE YOU GOING?

SHIRLEY AT COLLEGE HAS HER PARENTS' HOUSE ALL TO HERSELF. JEN AND I ARE MOVING IN TO KEEP HER COMPANY.

BUT CHRISTMAS IS A TIME FOR FAMILIES, ALISON.

SORRY. BUT MY MIND'S MADE UP.

SEEMS CHRISTMAS IS JUST ONE BIG HASSLE AROUND HERE, EH, MARTIN?

YEAH. IT'S A HASSLE ANYWAY, NOW WE'RE TOO OLD TO HANG UP STOCKINGS.

WHAT'S HAPPENING HERE? WHAT EVER HAPPENED TO THE SEASON OF GOODWILL AND ALL THAT STUFF?

It was pressie-wrapping time!

CRIKEY. MARTIN'S BOUGHT THESE WILD PATTERNED TIGHTS FOR MUM! MAYBE I SHOULD SWAP THEM FOR SOMETHING THAT'S MORE HER STYLE?

45

A NEW DIARY. ACE!
WELL, WE COULDN'T HAVE YOU WITHOUT ONE FOR NEXT YEAR, COULD WE, LOVE?

COME ON, YOU! TIME WE STARTED TO PREPARE THE VEG FOR DINNER.
YEOW! I'M COMING. I'M COMING.

And I had a nifty new typewriter too!
HEY, I COULD BE THE NEXT ENID BLYTON WITH THIS!

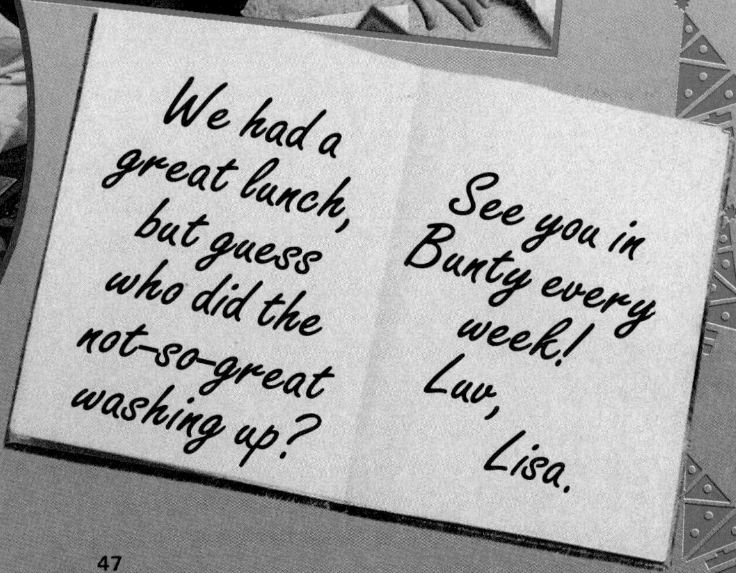
We had a great lunch, but guess who did the not-so-great washing up?
See you in Bunty every week! Luv, Lisa.

BUNTY – A girl like you

ENJOYING THE FILM, BUNTY?

WELL, I WOULD, JO, ONLY THE COUPLE BEHIND KEEP TALKING.

AND THE NOISE PEOPLE MAKE EATING SWEETS AND CRISPS.

IT'S TOTALLY OUT OF ORDER. I DON'T SEE WHY OUR SATURDAY NIGHTS OUT SHOULD BE RUINED.

Later that week —

WHAT'LL WE DO ON SATURDAY NIGHT? FANCY GOING TO THE CINEMA AGAIN?

NOT REALLY, JO.

ACTUALLY, I WAS GOING TO ASK IF YOU'D HELP ME BABYSIT MY TWO YOUNG COUSINS.

WELL . . . I DON'T KNOW, LISA. THOSE TWINS ARE A BIT OF A HANDFUL.

AW, PLEASE. WE CAN GET A VIDEO OUT AND WATCH A FILM IN PEACE FOR ONCE.

FAIR ENOUGH, THEN.

And so, on Saturday —

WE'LL GET THEM TO BED AND SIT AND WATCH OUR VIDEO.

NOW FOR SOME PEACE AND QUIET.

OH, NO! THEY'RE JUST NOT SETTLING AT ALL. I'LL HAVE TO BRING THEM DOWNSTAIRS.

HUH! SO MUCH FOR HAVING A NICE QUIET NIGHT IN TO WATCH OUR FILM!

DIARY OF HATE!

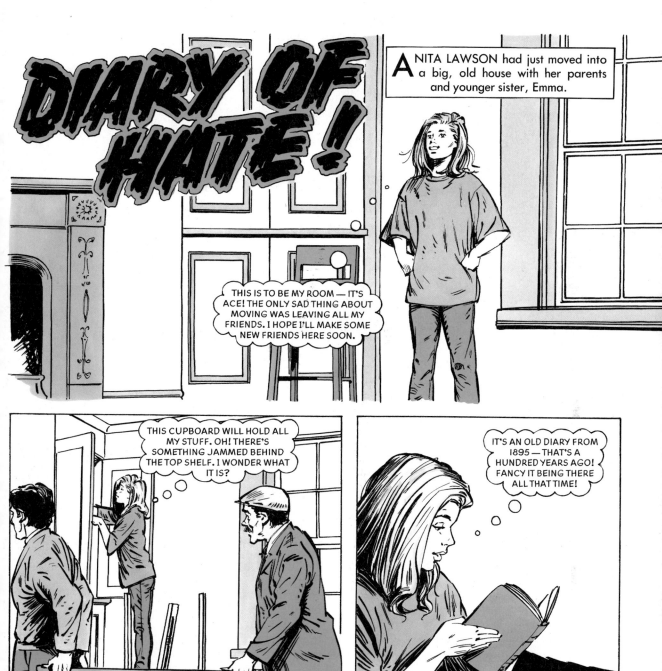

ANITA LAWSON had just moved into a big, old house with her parents and younger sister, Emma.

THIS IS TO BE MY ROOM — IT'S ACE! THE ONLY SAD THING ABOUT MOVING WAS LEAVING ALL MY FRIENDS. I HOPE I'LL MAKE SOME NEW FRIENDS HERE SOON.

THIS CUPBOARD WILL HOLD ALL MY STUFF. OH! THERE'S SOMETHING JAMMED BEHIND THE TOP SHELF. I WONDER WHAT IT IS?

IT'S AN OLD DIARY FROM 1895 — THAT'S A HUNDRED YEARS AGO! FANCY IT BEING THERE ALL THAT TIME!

"THIS IS THE DIARY OF ANNA LONGDEN, AGED 14. 3RD SEPTEMBER, 1895. TODAY WE MOVED INTO HOLLY LODGE."

THAT'S WEIRD! SHE MOVED IN HERE EXACTLY A HUNDRED YEARS AGO TODAY! AND SHE WAS FOURTEEN, LIKE ME. I WONDER IF SHE WAS HAPPY HERE?

Just then, Anita's mum called her downstairs.

I THOUGHT WE COULD HANG THESE PINK CURTAINS IN YOUR ROOM, ANITA.

NO! I'M *NOT* HAVING THEM! YOU KNOW I DON'T LIKE PINK! TAKE THEM AWAY — THEY'RE HORRIBLE!

OKAY, YOU WON'T GET THEM. LOOK, I KNOW IT'S HARD WORK SORTING EVERYTHING OUT, AND WE'RE ALL TIRED, BUT THERE'S NO NEED TO FLY OFF THE HANDLE LIKE THAT.

I'LL HAVE THEM, MUM — I LIKE PINK.

WHATEVER MADE ME ACT LIKE THAT? I WAS ROTTEN TO MUM. I SUPPOSE SHE WAS RIGHT — WE'RE ALL TIRED AND CRABBY. I'LL MAKE US ALL A COFFEE.

That night, Anita read the diary.

"I DON'T THINK I WILL BE HAPPY HERE. I DO NOT LIKE MY ROOM. EMILY'S IS MUCH NICER. MAMA TOLD ME I MUST HAVE AUNT MARIA'S ROCKING CHAIR IN MY ROOM, BUT I CRIED AND STAMPED MY FOOT UNTIL SHE CHANGED HER MIND."

THAT SOUNDS JUST LIKE WHAT HAPPENED TODAY WITH MUM AND THE PINK CURTAINS! ANNA CERTAINLY DIDN'T SEEM TO LIKE THE HOUSE TO START WITH. I WONDER IF SHE GOT TO LIKE IT LATER? I'LL READ SOME MORE TOMORROW.

Next day —

HI, THERE! YOU'VE JUST MOVED INTO HOLLY LODGE, HAVEN'T YOU? MY NAME'S KERRI. WOULD YOU LIKE ME TO SHOW YOU ROUND?

YES, PLEASE! AND MY NAME'S ANITA.

Later —

"MAMA MADE ME UNPACK ALL THE TOYS AND BOOKS TODAY. EMILY WOULD NOT HELP. SHE IS A NASTY, LAZY, LITTLE GIRL, SO I SHUT HER IN THE WARDROBE. SHE SCREAMED AND SCREAMED UNTIL NANNY LET HER OUT."

WHY — THAT'S EXACTLY WHAT HAPPENED TODAY TO ME AND EMMA! IT MUST JUST BE A COINCIDENCE. WE'RE NOT THE SAME — SHE DIDN'T LIKE IT HERE AND I LOVE THIS HOUSE!

The following evening —

I'LL TAKE SOME OF MY TAPES WITH ME TO KERRI'S HOUSE.

So —

HI, ANITA — COME AND MEET THE GANG.

LIKE A COKE, ANITA?

YES, PLEASE.

THEY ALL SEEM REALLY FRIENDLY.

But, later —

LOOK! ANITA'S GOT THE NEW "DANCE 95" TAPE! I'LL PUT IT ON NEXT.

NO! PUT IT DOWN! I ONLY GOT IT TODAY! I HAVEN'T HEARD IT YET AND I DON'T WANT ANYONE ELSE TO PLAY IT.

53

But, next morning —

YOU'RE SURELY NOT GOING TO THROW OUT THE OLD DIARY, ANITA? IT COULD BE VALUABLE. I'LL KEEP IT FOR YOU.

OH, NO! BUT IT'S NO USE TELLING MUM ABOUT IT — SHE'D NEVER BELIEVE THAT ANNA IS MAKING ME DO THINGS THAT SHE DID A HUNDRED YEARS AGO.

ARE YOU ALL RIGHT, LOVE? YOU FEEL A BIT HOT.

YES, MUM.

ACTUALLY, I'M NOT FEELING TOO GOOD. I WAS UP ALL NIGHT WORRYING ABOUT THE DIARY.

Soon —

I MUSTN'T TURN OUT LIKE ANNA. I'M SURE IF I'M CAREFUL I CAN STOP HER INFLUENCING ME.

ANITA! COULD YOU POST THIS LETTER FOR ME, DEAR?

NO, I DON'T HAVE TIME. YOU'LL HAVE TO DO IT YOURSELF!

OH!

At school —

I FEEL REALLY ASHAMED! HOW COULD I HAVE BEEN SO RUDE TO OUR NEIGHBOUR? IT MUST HAVE BEEN ANNA'S INFLUENCE WORKING ON ME AGAIN, EVEN THOUGH I WAS SURE I COULD STOP HER IF I TRIED. SHE'S TOO STRONG FOR ME! SHE'S BEGINNING TO TAKE ME OVER!

That night —

THAT'S STRANGE. THE DIARY ENDS QUITE SUDDENLY. PERHAPS SOMETHING HAPPENED TO ANNA. THERE MUST BE SOME WAY I CAN FIND OUT.

On Sunday —

ARE YOU SURE YOU WANT TO ATTEND CHURCH THIS MORNING, ANITA? YOU'VE HAD A TEMPERATURE THE LAST FEW DAYS.

YES, MUM.

I'VE HAD AN IDEA! MAYBE THERE'LL BE SOMETHING HERE ABOUT ANNA AND HER FAMILY. I'LL HAVE A LOOK ROUND THE TOMBSTONES.

ANNA LONGDEN
The beloved daughter of
HENRY and MARIA LONGDEN
who died on her fifteenth birthday
15th September 1895

THIS IS IT — ANNA'S GRAVESTONE! SHE DIED ON SEPTEMBER 15TH, 1895. THAT'S A HUNDRED YEARS AGO THIS WEEK AND IT'S MY FIFTEENTH BIRTHDAY, TOO! DOES ANNA WANT ME TO DIE ON MY BIRTHDAY?

Back home —

ANNA WAS VERY LONELY — MAYBE SHE WANTS ME TO BE WITH HER. WELL, I WON'T LET IT HAPPEN! I'LL ASK MUM IF I CAN HAVE A BIG PARTY ON THE 14TH. MAYBE ALL THE NOISE WILL DRIVE AWAY ANNA'S SPIRIT.

And so —

I STILL DON'T UNDERSTAND WHY YOU WANT YOUR PARTY TODAY, ANITA, INSTEAD OF TOMORROW.

MY BIRTHDAY WILL LAST LONGER IF THE PARTY'S TODAY, MUM.

I CAN'T TELL MUM THE REAL REASON — THAT I'M AFRAID IT MAY BE MY LAST BIRTHDAY. I'VE BEEN FEELING SO ILL RECENTLY — I JUST HOPE MY IDEA WORKS.

The COMP

A SPECIALLY WRITTEN STORY

OW! That hurt, Hodge! And what are you laughing at, Freddy? Hi, girls. Laura Brady here, nursing a sore neck from that paper pellet David flipping Hodgson just flicked at me. BOYS! Why are they all such a PAIN? And today Hodge and Freddy are being even worse than usual — which is going some!

It all started first thing, in Chemistry. When we went into the lab., Hodge was rabbiting on as usual — about how useless girls are at science, how all great scientists are men, yak, yak, etc.

"Name one great woman scientist," he challenged us.

"Marie Curie," I said.

"Never heard of her," smirked Freddy. "That proves it."

"No, it proves all boys are thick," said Becky sweetly.

Well, we had to do an experiment with sulphur. It was SUPPOSED to smell. But I'm not sure it was supposed to smell quite as bad as the lump of green stuff me and Becky produced. I mean, imagine rotten eggs, school shepherd's pie, your brother's smelliest old trainers — worse than that lot mixed! Of course, Hodge and Freddy went RIGHT over the top with the fuss they made.

"FWAW! Worrapong! Gimme air!"

"ARRGGGH! Help me! I'm suffocating!"

No such luck.

"It's SUPPOSED to whiff," Becky growled. "It shows us girls have done the experiment properly!"

Even Mr Lewis, the Chemistry teacher, agreed that this was the case. But it didn't stop Hodge and Freddy from following us round the playground all break, holding their noses and pretending to pass out, which got us well and truly ratty.

"Boys!" I snorted. "Who needs 'em!"

"Me," said Hayley dreamily. Hayley is Becky's twin, and right then she had stars in her eyes — not 'cos of that horrible pair Hodge and Freddy, I hasten to add, but because Dreamboat Darren Palmer had just walked by. Darren's in the fifth year and he thinks he's gorgeous. Trouble was, Hayley agreed with him.

"If only he'd notice me!" she sighed.

"Like he'd notice a mere third year," grinned Roz. "I reckon it's Marilyn Smith he fancies!"

Marilyn Smith's a fourth year, and she IS pretty. I mean, REALLY pretty. She's modelled and stuff. But she's okay with it. I have to admit, if Darren was going to look at any mere schoolgirl, it'd be someone like her. But Hayley went on walking round with stars in her eyes, which made her an easy target for Hodge and Freddy's next trick. They waited till she was sitting in the canteen, toying with her cheese salad and gazing dreamily at Darren in the distance — and then they walked by her table.

"EEEK!" Hayley was up and dancing, her plate was upside-down on the floor and there was a huge, hairy spider in her drinking water!

Hodge and Freddy were crying with laughter. Boys! They're all brain dead. I mean, fake spiders. How corny can you get? I bet they spend all their pocket money in the joke shop.

That's why, after lunch, me and Becky thrashed those two at knockabout football. If there's one thing they hate, it's being beaten by a couple of mere girls! We scored more goals than they did

AND I saved some of Hodge's best shots — which didn't please him too much!

And that's why I'm getting this barrage of paper pellets from them now, in Maths. OUCH! That one stung!

"LAURA BRADY!"

Uh, oh! Basher Bartlett, the mad Maths teacher!

"MUST you keep making those ridiculous yapping noises, girl? You're disturbing your classmates!"

ME! ME disturbing THEM! Look at those two snorting with silent laughter . . . you wait. I'll — I'll cook rock cakes in Food Tech and make 'em EAT 'em. THAT'LL serve 'em right!

Later, Hayley came rushing over — and she's in seventh heaven. "He's done it!" she gasped. "Darren! He's asked me out — on a date — tonight!"

You could've knocked me down with half a feather. I never honestly thought he would. I thought Roz was right — as if Mr I'm-So-Wonderful would ever notice a third year.

But he HAD!

Roz was dead envious. "Wow! Lucky you!" she breathed. "He is drop-dead GORGEOUS!"

All right — if I'm honest, she wasn't the only envious one. Quite a few of us wouldn't have minded a cosy evening at Luigi's Pizza Parlour, with Darren Palmer.

But then Hodge and Freddy came over. As if I hadn't already had enough of those two for one day!

"Laura," Hodge said. "Can we have a word?"

"How about dork?" I suggested. "Or thickhead? Or . . ."

"No, we're serious," Freddy said. And they did look it. They drew Becky and me aside. "What's up?" I asked.

Hodge looked a bit uncomfortable. "It's like this. We think we ought to warn you . . ." He glanced at Freddy.

"It's Darren Palmer," said Freddy. "We just heard him . . . come and hear for yourself."

They led us to where Darren was holding court with a few of his mates. We hid nearby and listened. It wasn't hard to hear what he was saying. He was so pleased with himself, he wasn't bothering to keep his voice down.

"You're kidding, Darren!" one

of his mates was chortling. "You've asked a third year out?"

"Get real," Darren grinned. "I happen to know Marilyn Smith's going to be at Luigi's tonight — she's got a job there waiting tables!"

His mates all laughed. "Going to get Marilyn interested by parading another girl in front of her?"

"What else do you think I'd need a third year kid for?" smirked Darren. "But she's crazy about me, so I might as well make use of her! Why don't you guys turn up and see the fun?"

The CREEP! Becky and I were BOILING! Hodge and Freddy drew us away before we rushed out and confronted that toerag!

"Poor Hayley!" breathed Becky angrily.

"Thought you ought to know," said Hodge.

"Thanks," I said. "Now just let us go and KILL him!"

"No, hang on," Freddy said. "We've got a better idea."

It WAS, too! Those two can really come up with the goods sometimes!

The hard part was breaking it to Hayley. She was upset, natch. But when we told her the boys' plan, she slowly began to cheer up. And by the evening she was even looking forward to it.

It's seven-fifteen, and Becky, Roz and I are hiding round the corner from Luigi's, waiting for the fun to begin. Darren Palmer is outside Luigi's with his mates — and he's starting to look uneasy, because Hayley should have been there quarter of an hour ago.

"Been stood up, Darren?" grinned one of his mates.

"Nah, do me a favour," snorts Darren. "She'll be along!"

He wasn't wrong. At that moment she turned up — arm in

arm with Freddy! "Oh! Hello, Darren!" she says, all surprised. "Fancy seeing YOU here!"

Darren's face was a picture! "Here — we had a date!" he gasps.

"In your dreams!" says Hayley, and she and Freddy walk off, all smoochy!

Darren's mates are falling about! Darren looks like he could kill the lot of them! But then suddenly, Marilyn walks up, looking stunning. And Darren forgets all about Hayley. He's drooling!

"Hi, there," says Marilyn, fluttering her eyelashes. "It's my night off. You free?"

Darren can't believe his luck! He thinks it's his birthday!

"You bet, doll!"

"Shame," says Marilyn sweetly. "'Cos I'M not!" and up walks Hodge and she slips an arm through his.

"Bye, bye, Darren!" she says. "And did I mention, I wouldn't be seen dead with you if you were the only guy in Redvale?" And she walks off with Hodge!

I told you Marilyn was a decent sort. When we told her what Darren was planning to do, she was only too pleased to help take the bighead down a peg or two! Oh, boy, I wish I'd had a camera — mind you, Darren's expression right then would have cracked the lens!

And we all — Hodge, Freddy, Marilyn, Hayley, Becky, Roz and me — wound up having a brill time down at the bowling alley. You know, come to think of it, I suppose ALL boys aren't so bad after all. One or two of 'em can be quite human at times — like Hodge and Freddy.

What's that, Hodge? Did you just say girls can't bowl for toffee? Excuse me, girls. I've just got to go and prove him WRONG!

THE END

Storm

GOOD BOY, PATCH! YOU'RE JUMPING NICELY NOW.

AMANDA ELLIS'S father was a horse dealer, and Amanda loved to ride the different horses and ponies he had in the yard.

THAT'S ENOUGH FOR NOW. IT'S TIME FOR YOUR LUNCH. DAD'S GOT SOMEONE COMING TO TRY YOU THIS AFTERNOON.

I LIKE PATCH, BUT HE'S A GOOD, RELIABLE PONY, AND DAD WILL SOON FIND A BUYER FOR HIM.

HELLO, TRIXIE. I HAVEN'T FORGOTTEN YOU. I'LL BRING YOU SOME LUNCH IN A MINUTE, TOO.

TRIXIE'S THE ONLY PONY DAD WON'T EVER SELL. SHE'S OLD NOW, BUT I LEARNED TO RIDE ON HER. PERHAPS ONE DAY THERE'LL BE ANOTHER PONY DAD WILL LET ME HAVE AS MY OWN.

HERE'S DAD, BACK FROM THE SALE. I WONDER IF HE'S BOUGHT ANY NEW HORSES?

WHATEVER HAVE YOU BOUGHT, DAD? IT'S MAKING A TERRIFIC RACKET IN THERE!

YES, IT'S A BIT OF A WILD ONE THIS TIME, AMANDA, BUT WE MAY BE ABLE TO MAKE SOMETHING OF HIM. HE WAS CHEAP, SO I THOUGHT IT WAS WORTH THE RISK. STAND CLEAR WHILE I BRING HIM OUT.

The Perfect Partner

DANIELLE BOND was just leaving school one day —

HOME TIME. BRILLIANT! THERE'S MARC WAITING FOR ME. WE'VE GOT A PRACTICE ON.

HE'S GORGEOUS, DANIELLE. I WISH THERE WAS A BOY LIKE THAT WAITING FOR *ME!*

HE'S JUST MY DISCO DANCING PARTNER. WE'RE GOOD MATES, THAT'S ALL.

HI, MARC.

HI, DANIELLE. COME ON, WE WANT A REALLY GOOD PRACTICE SESSION TODAY. IT'S NOT LONG UNTIL OUR NEXT COMPETITION.

Soon —

...AND UP! LOVELY!

Afterwards —

WELL DONE, BOTH OF YOU. I'M SURE YOU'RE GOING TO DO REALLY WELL IN THE COMPETITION.

THAT WAS BRILLIANT. I LOVE DANCING SO MUCH, AND SO DOES MARC.

66

In town —

DANIELLE! I HOPED I'D SEE YOU TODAY. I'VE GOT SOMETHING TO TELL YOU.

MARC!

But —

I WANT YOU TO MEET ZOE. SHE'S MY NEW GIRLFRIEND. ZOE, THIS IS DANIELLE, MY DANCING PARTNER.

HI, DANIELLE. MARC'S TOLD ME ALL ABOUT YOU.

ER — HI, ZOE.

BUT I DIDN'T KNOW ANYTHING ABOUT *YOU*! I THOUGHT MARC DIDN'T WANT A GIRLFRIEND AND THAT'S WHY HE DIDN'T ASK ME OUT!

I'LL JUST HAVE TO CONCENTRATE ON DANCING FROM NOW ON. I WON'T EVEN THINK ABOUT ZOE — THOUGH IT'S GOING TO BE HARD.

At the next session —

EVEN DANCING'S NOT THE SAME ANY MORE. ZOE COMES TO WATCH MARC ALL THE TIME. SHE'S GOING TO COME TO OUR NEXT COMPETITION, TOO.

MARC ONLY WANTS ME AS A DANCING PARTNER NOW. WE WOULD USUALLY HAVE GONE OFF FOR A COKE OR SOMETHING TOGETHER AFTER PRACTICE. I MISS HIM AS A FRIEND, NEVER MIND ANYTHING ELSE.

I CAN'T BEAR IT! I'LL HAVE TO GO ROUND TO MARC'S HOUSE TOMORROW AND SPEAK TO HIM. THERE'S NOTHING ELSE FOR IT.

So, next day —

NOT BE MY PARTNER ANY MORE? BUT WHY, DANIELLE? WE'RE GREAT TOGETHER.

IT'S JUST THE WAY I FEEL, MARC. I DON'T WANT TO DANCE WITH YOU ANY MORE.

WELL, IF YOU'RE SURE, DANIELLE . . .

I MANAGED TO CONVINCE HIM IN THE END. AND HERE COMES ZOE NOW. OH, I'M SO MISERABLE.

A few days later, at dance class —

HEY, WHAT'S THIS ABOUT YOU AND MARC? IS IT TRUE YOU'RE NOT HIS PARTNER ANY MORE?

ER — YES. I JUST DIDN'T WANT TO DANCE WITH HIM ANY MORE, THAT'S ALL.

COME ON, DANIELLE. LOOSEN UP. YOU CAN DO BETTER THAN THIS.

I CAN'T. I FEEL ALL WOODEN.

At the end of the class —

POOR DANIELLE — SHE'S UPSET. SHE CAN'T DANCE PROPERLY NOW SHE HAS NO PARTNER.

LYN'S RIGHT AND I'D BETTER DO SOMETHING ABOUT IT. I'LL PUT IN SOME EXTRA TRAINING.

So, the next evening —

I'D BETTER DO PLENTY OF WARM-UP EXERCISES, THEN I'M GOING TO WORK ON A NEW ROUTINE.

Secret Schoolgirl

CONTINUED FROM PAGE 20

RUNAWAY, Amy Howard, was back with her old friends at Blackstone Academy. Next morning —

YOU'D BETTER STAY HERE, AMY, AND WE'LL SMUGGLE UP SOME BREAKFAST FOR YOU. YOU SHOULD BE OKAY UNTIL THE CLEANING LADY COMES ROUND.

DON'T WORRY ABOUT ME. I'LL KEEP OUT OF SIGHT. THANKS FOR YOUR HELP.

Later —

YOU'LL HAVE TO HIDE SOMEWHERE ELSE, AMY! MATRON'S COMING INTO ALL THE ROOMS ON THIS CORRIDOR THIS MORNING TO MEASURE UP FOR NEW CURTAINS.

WE THOUGHT YOU COULD HIDE IN THE DRAMA STOREROOM DURING THE DAY. WE'LL BRING YOU SOME FOOD AND MAGS TO READ.

AND SOME SCHOOL BOOKS, TOO. I'VE STILL GOT MY EDUCATION TO KEEP UP, REMEMBER.

THIS IS A GREAT HIDING-PLACE. I CAN HIDE IN THOSE BIG CUPBOARDS IF ANYONE COMES.

I CAN'T STAY FOR EVER, AND I DON'T WANT MY FRIENDS TO GET INTO TROUBLE FOR HELPING ME. BUT WHERE CAN I GO? ONE THING'S FOR SURE — I'M NOT GOING BACK TO AUNTIE BETTY.

WHAT'S THAT? I HEAR VOICES.

71

THIS IS GREAT. I CAN HEAR MY CLASS IN THEIR LESSON. WHAT A PIECE OF LUCK.

OH! THERE'S SOMEONE COMING! I'D BETTER HIDE!

WOW! LOOK AT THIS LOT! WE'RE SURE TO FIND SOMETHING HERE THAT'LL SCARE THOSE STUPID FIRST YEAR KIDS.

GREAT! I'M SURE THEY BELIEVE ALL THOSE GHOST STORIES WE'VE BEEN TELLING THEM ABOUT THE VEILED LADY WHO FLOATS DOWN THE STAIRS AT FULL MOON.

WHAT ABOUT THIS DRESS? I COULD WEAR IT WITH THAT CLOAK AND A BIT OF NET FOR A VEIL.

WHAT A ROTTEN TRICK. VERA AND MADGE ARE A NASTY PAIR. THEY'RE ALWAYS TRYING TO STIR THINGS UP. WELL — THIS COULD BE MY CHANCE TO PLAY A TRICK ON THEM! IF I CAN HIT THAT HAT . . .

HEY! WHAT ARE YOU DOING?

IT WASN'T ME! I DIDN'T TOUCH ANYTHING.

IT'S CREEPY IN HERE! LET'S FORGET THE VEILED LADY, VERA. IT WAS A ROTTEN IDEA ANYWAY.

YEAH! I'M GETTING OUT OF HERE.

I DON'T THINK THOSE TWO WILL BE PLAYING ANY MORE NASTY TRICKS ON THE JUNIORS.

At lunchtime —

I'M PLAYING IN A HOCKEY MATCH THIS AFTERNOON. IT'S THE FIRST TIME I'VE BEEN PICKED FOR THE TEAM AND I'M SURE TO MAKE A MESS OF IT. I WISH YOU WERE STILL CAPTAIN, AMY.

DON'T WORRY, JANE! ONCE YOU'RE OUT ON THE FIELD YOU WON'T BE NERVOUS.

I KNOW, AMY. I JUST WISH YOU WERE PLAYING, THAT'S ALL.

That afternoon —

OH, NO! JANE! HOW COULD YOU MISS?

I'M HOPELESS! WE'LL NEVER WIN NOW. I JUST WISH THE GAME WAS OVER!

COME ON, JANE! YOU CAN DO IT!

THAT'S AMY SHOUTING. SHE'S DRESSED UP IN COSTUMES FROM THE DRAMA STOREROOM. SHE COULD BE IN BIG TROUBLE IF SHE'S RECOGNISED, BUT SHE STILL CAME TO CHEER ME ON! I'LL HAVE TO KEEP TRYING.

GREAT GOAL, JANE.

I'D NEVER HAVE DONE IT IF AMY HADN'T BEEN HERE.

That night, Amy was smuggled back into the girls' dormitory —

I'M SURE MUM AND DAD WOULD LET YOU COME AND LIVE WITH US, AMY. DO YOU THINK YOUR AUNT WOULD AGREE?

I DON'T KNOW, NINA . . .

SHH-HH! HIDE, AMY! I THINK SOMEONE'S COMING!

IT'S TIME FOR LIGHTS-OUT, GIRLS. BY THE WAY, MAKE SURE YOUR ROOM IS TIDY IN THE MORNING. A NEW GIRL WILL BE MOVING IN WITH YOU TOMORROW.

OH, NO! THAT MEANS I WON'T BE ABLE TO SLEEP IN HERE AGAIN. AND IT'LL BE HARDER FOR THE OTHERS TO HELP ME IF THERE'S SOMEONE ELSE HANGING AROUND.

YOU'LL HAVE TO STAY IN THE DRAMA STOREROOM ALL THE TIME IF WE HAVE A NEW GIRL IN HERE. BUT DON'T WORRY! WE WON'T LET ANYONE FIND OUT YOU'RE HERE.

THANKS! YOU'RE THE BEST PALS ANYONE COULD HAVE.

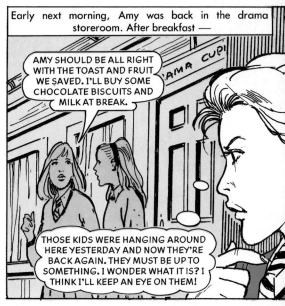

Early next morning, Amy was back in the drama storeroom. After breakfast —

AMY SHOULD BE ALL RIGHT WITH THE TOAST AND FRUIT WE SAVED. I'LL BUY SOME CHOCOLATE BISCUITS AND MILK AT BREAK.

THOSE KIDS WERE HANGING AROUND HERE YESTERDAY AND NOW THEY'RE BACK AGAIN. THEY MUST BE UP TO SOMETHING. I WONDER WHAT IT IS? I THINK I'LL KEEP AN EYE ON THEM!

Some time later —

OH, NO! I'VE LEFT MY BAG IN THE DORMITORY! I'LL HAVE TO GO BACK FOR IT — THE OTHERS COULD BE IN REAL TROUBLE IF SOMEONE FINDS IT AND STARTS ASKING AWKWARD QUESTIONS.

CONTINUED ON PAGE 97

THE *BEST* BEST FRIEND?

Are you a brilliant best buddy or the kind of pal a gal could do without? Wanna find out? Then answer these easy peasy questions . . .

1. *Your best mate and your boyfriend don't get on at all. What do you do?*

a) Chuck him — no boy is worth losing your best pal.
b) Try to see them both, but at separate times.
c) Tell her she'll have to get used to him.

2. *It's your birthday. What do you expect from your best friend?*

b) Whatever she can afford. She always thinks of something nice anyway.
c) Oh, just the usual — pressies, flowers, chocolates, etc.
a) Nothing much. It's no big deal.

3. *Your best friend has spent all day trying out a new look for her hair. The results are a disaster. What do you say?*

a) You say you like it.
b) You suggest another idea (anything would be better).
c) Laugh your head off.

4. *There's a school trip to the new theme park coming up but only one place remains — what do you do?*

a) Insist that your best mate goes and tell her not to worry about you.
b) Decide to both miss out — you can always work at persuading one of your parents to take you instead.
c) Tell her if she goes without you, you'll never speak to her again.

5. *Your best friend's boyfriend asks you out. What do you do?*

c) Tell him he'll have to dump her first. You're not sharing him with anyone.
b) Tell him to get lost and hope she dumps him soon.
a) Tell her he's asked you out so that they split up immediately — you don't like to share your best friend with anyone, anyway.

6. *Your best mate has gone on holiday and didn't send you a postcard. What is your reaction?*

c) Who cares? As long as she remembers to bring back a present!
b) You reckon she must be really enjoying herself!
a) You are heartbroken and go in a huff.

7. *It's the end of term party. Your pal can't go because she's got a throat infection. She's been off all week. Do you —*

b) Go round with a card and some chocs to cheer her up then go to the party so you can keep up to date with all the latest news.
c) Hit the party in full swing.
a) Stay in with your pal and miss out on the party.

8. *You hear that your best friend has been gossiping about you. What do you do?*

c) Spread some equally horrid gossip about her.
a) Say nothing — it can't be true.
b) Ask her about it — there's two sides to every story.

9. *You've had an argument with your best friend. How do you make up?*

b) Say you're sorry and decide to forget about it.
a) Buy her a pressie, say you're sorry and you'll do her homework for her!
c) Wait for *her* to apologise of course.

10. *The school bullies have a go at your best mate. What do you do?*

c) Nothing. It's her problem.
b) Advise her to get help from a teacher or tell her parents.
a) Decide you'd both better keep out of the bullies' way.

11. *Your best mate is half an hour late meeting you. What do you do?*

a) Go home in a huff.
b) Go home and call her to find out what the problem is.
c) Storm round to her house and demand an explanation.

12. *Your best pal wants you to go swimming with her 3 times a week. You're not too keen. What do you say?*

b) Say you'll go once a week with her.
a) Agree to go and hope she goes off the idea soon.
c) Inform her that you're not a fish and refuse.

13. *A new girl joins your class and starts tagging along with you and your best pal. How do you feel?*

a) Worried she might be taking your best friend away.
b) Pleased to meet someone new.
c) Annoyed. Three's a crowd!

CONCLUSIONS

Mostly A's
You are a very loyal and devoted best friend but maybe you worry too much about losing your mate. Also, try to think of yourself from time to time and relax!

Mostly B's
You are a sensible, level-headed best friend that any girl would be lucky to have. You are honest and try your best.

Mostly C's
You are great fun to be with and always a good laugh but you should be more considerate and think of others more instead of yourself.

PARTLY, BUT HER PERSONALITY HAS CHANGED. SHE KNOWS SHE IS A LADY AND IS BEHAVING LIKE A SPOILED BRAT. HOPEFULLY, SHE WILL RECOVER NOW THAT SHE IS BACK AMONG FRIENDS.

I UNDERSTAND, HEADMISTRESS.

In the study the Marys shared —

MESSAGE FOR YOU, FROM RADDY. SHE'S AT THE MAIN ENTRANCE AND SHE WANTS YOU TO CARRY HER BAGS.

HA! HA! WHAT A JOKER SHE IS!

The Marys waited for Raddy to appear. At last —

HERE SHE IS! WELCOME BACK, RADDY. YOU ARE A TEASE!

TEASE? I WASN'T TEASING! I SUMMONED YOU!

WHEN YOU DIDN'T COME, I HAD TO GET SOMEONE ELSE TO CARRY MY BAGS. PUT THEM DOWN THERE, JENNY, AND HERE'S A POUND FOR YOU.

MY GOODNESS, RADDY. YOU ARE PLAYING THE LADY!

I AM A LADY. KINDLY REMEMBER THAT IN FUTURE, AND ADDRESS ME AS LADY MARY — AND NOT BY SOME RIDICULOUS NICKNAME. NOW I'M GOING TO SEE WHAT'S HAPPENED TO MY TEA. YOU THREE CAN START MY UNPACKING!

SHE'S TAKING THIS JOKE A BIT FAR, ISN'T SHE?

I'M NOT SURE IT IS A JOKE, COTTY. FOR SOME REASON, I THINK RADDY'S BECOME A SNOB!

Later —

MY TAPE'S FINISHED. CHANGE IT OVER, SIMPSON.

YOU COULD TRY SAYING "PLEASE."

DON'T TELL *ME* WHAT TO DO! IF YOU DON'T LIKE SHARING A STUDY WITH ME, ASK FOR A TRANSFER. I'M QUITE SURE OTHER PUPILS WILL BE QUEUEING UP TO ROOM WITH A MEMBER OF THE ARISTOCRACY.

IF SHE KEEPS GOING ON LIKE THIS, THEY WON'T.

But two people were *very* interested in being friendly with the new Radleigh — the third year snobs, Mabel and Veronica!

RADLEIGH'S COME TO HER SENSES AT LAST, MABEL. SHE'S FINALLY REALISED THOSE OTHER MARYS ARE BENEATH HER.

I'VE ALWAYS THOUGHT WE SHOULD MIX WITH THE ARISTOCRACY, VERONICA. LET'S GO AND INVITE HER TO OUR STUDY.

WHERE ARE YOU GOING, RADDY?

LADY MARY IS COMING TO OUR STUDY.

WHAT? BUT WE DON'T EVEN LIKE MABEL AND VERONICA!

YOU MAY NOT, BUT I FIND THEM VERY AGREEABLE COMPANIONS.

THAT'S TELLING THEM, LADY MARY!

The following day —

RADDY'S HARDLY SAID TWO WORDS TO US. SHE SPENDS ALL HER TIME WITH THE SNOBS NOW.

Then —

I NEED FOUR PEOPLE TO CATALOGUE SOME NEW BOOKS FOR THE LIBRARY. RADLEIGH, SIMPSON, FIELD AND COTTER CAN DO IT.

ONCE WE'D HAVE HAD FUN WORKING TOGETHER — BUT NOT ANY MORE. OH, WELL. BETTER MAKE THE BEST OF IT.

THIS JOB SHOULDN'T BE TOO BAD. AT LEAST WE'LL GET TO SEE THE NEW BOOKS FIRST.

I THINK IT SOUNDS VERY TIRESOME. I WOULD NEVER HAD AGREED TO DO SUCH A MENIAL TASK — EXCEPT THAT IT GETS ME OFF PREP. NOT THAT I INTEND TO DO ANY ACTUAL WORK.

I SHALL SIT HERE AND READ. YOU THREE CAN DO THE CATALOGUING.

NOW LOOK HERE . . .

LEAVE IT, COTTY.

PASS ME THAT BIG VOLUME NEXT, COTTY.

HERE IT COMES.

AAH! I'VE DROPPED IT!

OOH! RADDY'S HEAD.

AAGH!

WE'LL FIND PLACES FOR AS MANY AS POSSIBLE, OF COURSE — BUT I'M AFRAID THERE WILL ONLY BE ONE SOLUTION FOR THOSE WE CAN'T PLACE.

YOU MEAN THEY'LL HAVE TO BE PUT TO SLEEP? OH, MRS LAWSON, NO — WE MUST SAVE THEM SOMEHOW! COULDN'T WE ASK THE LOCAL PAPER TO HELP, BY RUNNING THE STORY, AND ADVERTISE FOR HOMES IN LOCAL SHOPS?

YES, BUT WE MUST FACE FACTS, CARLY. SOME OF OUR CATS ARE HERE SIMPLY BECAUSE NO-ONE WANTS THEM — PATCH, WITH HIS LAME LEG, TANSY WHO HASN'T EATEN PROPERLY SINCE HER OWNER DIED — EVEN GOOD OLD GRISELDA, WHO IS SO INDEPENDENT.

AND THERE'S THE WILD KITTENS, TOO. BUT WE'LL FIND THEM HOMES, MRS LAWSON. WE MUST!

The other helpers were as keen as Carly to find homes for the cats—

I'LL ASK MY MUM. SHE WORKS IN THE NEWSAGENT'S.

I'LL ASK AT SCHOOL AS WELL. SOME OF THE TEACHERS MIGHT BE INTERESTED.

AND WE COULD PUT UP A BIG NOTICE OUTSIDE THE GATES HERE. PASSERS-BY MIGHT COME IN.

THAT WAS MRS HATTON-HALL ON THE PHONE. SHE SAYS THERE IS A 'GREY ANIMAL' DIGGING IN HER GARDEN, AND WOULD WE COLLECT IT BEFORE SHE TAKES A BROOM TO IT. I'M AFRAID IT'LL BE GRISELDA. SHE DOES SEEM TO LIKE NEXT DOOR'S GARDEN.

I'LL GET HER.

WHAT A SHAME MRS HATTON-HALL DOESN'T LIKE CATS. THOSE OUTBUILDINGS NEXT TO THE HOUSE WOULD BE PERFECT FOR THE SANCTUARY. I WONDER IF IT'S WORTH MENTIONING IT TO HER? AFTER ALL, WE'D PAY HER RENT.

86

But, as Carly went down the street—

TANG!

OH, NO! I DIDN'T FASTEN THE STRAP PROPERLY. IF HE PANICS I'LL NEVER CATCH HIM!

TANG, COME BACK!

HE'S GONE IN THAT WINDOW. I HOPE HE DOESN'T CAUSE ANY DAMAGE. THE SANCTUARY'S IN ENOUGH TROUBLE ALREADY.

But—

OH — YOU'VE GOT HIM! SORRY, HE GOT OUT OF HIS BASKET.

SO HE BELONGS TO YOU? I WAS HOPING HE WAS A STRAY. IT WAS LIKE A SCENE FROM ONE OF MY OWN STORIES. HE CAME IN THROUGH THE WINDOW AND JUMPED STRAIGHT ON TO THE TOP OF MY WORD PROCESSOR — JUST AS MY DEAR OLD CAT USED TO DO.

YOU MEAN, YOU REALLY WANT A CAT? TANG NEEDS A HOME. I CAN SEE YOU'RE A CAT PERSON — AND TANG KNOWS IT AS WELL. WOULD YOU LIKE TO HAVE HIM?

I'D BE DELIGHTED! I'VE HARDLY BEEN ABLE TO WRITE A THING SINCE MY JASON WAS RUN OVER. CATS ARE WONDERFUL COMPANIONS.

Then, as Carly headed for home—

CARLY — GUESS WHAT? I WAS GOING TO DO A BIT OF FISHING IN THE CANAL, AND I SAW THIS COUPLE ON A BARGE CHASE A RAT OFF THEIR BOAT. WE GOT TALKING — AND THEY SAID THEY'LL TAKE ALL THREE OF OUR WILD KITTENS. THEY DON'T MIND COPING WITH THEM A BIT.

THAT'S GREAT, JAMES. AND TANG'S FOUND A HOME AS WELL.

88

Christmas CRACKERS

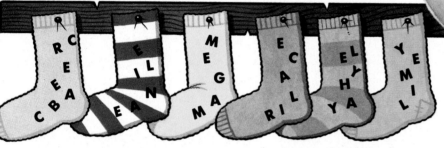

Word Up!

Turn YULE into TIDE in FOUR steps, changing one letter each time to make a new word!

YULE

- - - -

- - - -

- - - -

TIDE

TALKING STOCKINGS!

Six Bunty readers have hung their stockings here. Each stocking has the name of its owner on the front — but the letters have become jumbled up. Can you puzzle it out?

Fairy Fay

Only two of these fairies are original Fairy Fays. These two match. The others are impostors. Can you find the genuine ones? Get puzzling!

A

B

C

D

CELEBRITY SANTA!

Who is this cunningly disguised mega star Santa?

NAME - - - - - -   - - - - - - - - - - - - -

SECRET PUDDING

Inside the scrummy Christmas pudding you'll find all its ingredients hiding and loadsa other tasty Christmas treats!

BREADCRUMBS
ICE CREAM
RAISINS
CURRANTS
FLOUR
SUGAR
BUTTER
PEEL
SUET
SPICES
TREACLE
ICING
CREAM
TRIFLE
PIES
CHOCS
MINTS
CAKE
NUTS

O	I	V	S	O	T		
M	G	N	T	B	T	R	S	O
D	A	V	N	P	R	S	I	E	R	N
A	F	E	A	G	I	E	E	F	P	S	M
R	E	E	R	T	R	E	A	C	L	E	N	I	I
B	D	R	C	E	O	S	D	I	E	E	I	N	W
E	U	U	E	A	T	E	C	P	E	L	S	T	O
C	H	O	C	S	V	T	R	S	C	K	I	S	T
S	A	L	I	R	A	G	U	S	R	T	A	S
R	E	F	M	E	N	N	M	B	E	V	R	C
O	A	N	U	I	B	U	A	I	O	M
T	U	T	C	S	E	M	L	T
Y	S	I	U	L	E	E

ANSWERS

WORD UP — yule, rule, rude, ride, tide or yule, yale, tale, tile, tide.
CELEBRITY SANTA — It's Arnold Schwarzenegger.
TALKING STOCKINGS — Rebecca, Elaine, Gemma, Claire, Hayley, Emily.
FAIRY FAY — A, D.

90

The COMP

IT was nearly the end of the Christmas term at Redvale Comp. One morning —

NOT LONG NOW! ONLY A FEW MORE DAYS OF TORTURE TO GO!

HEY, MAYBE THE BUS WON'T GET THROUGH THE SNOW AND THEN WE'LL GET TODAY OFF SCHOOL!

NO SUCH LUCK, ROZ! HERE IT COMES!

HOPE THE SNOW LASTS TILL CHRISTMAS. IT ALWAYS FEELS MORE LIKE CHRISTMAS WHEN IT'S SNOWING.

Suddenly —

THE BUS IS SKIDDING!

LAURA!

AAH!

SORRY. I COULDN'T HELP IT — WE HIT AN ICY PATCH. HOW'S THE GIRL?

SHE'S UNCONSCIOUS. WE'D BETTER GET AN AMBULANCE!

91

OH, POOR LAURA!

SHE HIT HER HEAD HARD. I SURE HOPE SHE'LL BE OKAY.

Soon —

WHERE . . . WHERE AM I?

LIE STILL NOW. YOU'RE IN HOSPITAL, LAURA. YOU HAD A BIT OF AN ACCIDENT — CAN YOU REMEMBER HOW IT HAPPENED?

NO. OW, MY HEAD HURTS!

CONCUSSION. WE'LL KEEP HER IN A COUPLE OF DAYS FOR OBSERVATION. TAKE HER TO THE GENERAL WARD, NURSE.

Later, at school —

GET TO YOUR CLASSES, GIRLS! THE BELL WENT TEN MINUTES AGO!

PLEASE, MISS GRIMSTYLE — HAVE YOU HEARD ANY NEWS ABOUT LAURA YET?

LAURA BRADY IS BEING WELL TAKEN CARE OF. SHE IS IN THE BEST PLACE. NOW, YOU HAVE WORK TO DO. IT'S NOT THE HOLIDAYS YET!

HOW CAN GRIM GERTIE BE SUCH A MONSTER?

Later —

HELLO! YOU'VE HAD A NAP. I'VE BEEN WAITING FOR YOU TO WAKE UP! I'M ALICE. WHO ARE YOU?

I — I'M LAURA.

OH! SHE'S IN A WHEELCHAIR.

NURSE JUNE SAID YOU'VE GOT CON-CONFUSION. WHAT'S THAT? DO YOU WANT TO PLAY A GAME? I'VE GOT LOTS.

NOW, ALICE, DON'T PESTER POOR LAURA!

NO, I DON'T MIND. I'D LIKE TO PLAY, ALICE.

And so —

I'VE WON!

YOU'RE FAR TOO GOOD FOR ME!

YOUR GRAN'S HERE TO SEE YOU, ALICE. OFF YOU GO!

ARE YOU BETTER, DEAR? THE DOCTOR SAID YOU CAN REMEMBER YOUR ACCIDENT NOW.

YES, I'M FINE. NURSE JUNE, WHAT HAPPENED TO ALICE?

IT WAS VERY SAD. SHE WAS PARALYSED IN A CAR CRASH SIX MONTHS AGO. SHE LOST BOTH HER PARENTS BUT SHE'LL BE LEAVING HERE SOON — GOING HOME TO HER GRAN.

That evening —

CAN WE SEE LAURA BRADY, PLEASE? WE'RE HER BEST FRIENDS.

OF COURSE. LAURA'S MUCH BETTER — WE'LL BE LETTING HER OUT TOMORROW.

OOPS!

ALICE! WATCH IT, YOU LITTLE SPEED MERCHANT! YOU'RE A DANGER TO OTHER ROAD USERS!

HA! HA! SORRY!

I SEE YOU'VE MET OUR ALICE! ISN'T SHE AMAZING?

SHE'S CERTAINLY NIPPY IN THAT CHAIR! LIKE A RACING DRIVER!

SHE WON'T HAVE IT FOR MUCH LONGER, THOUGH.

WHAT DO YOU MEAN?

WELL, WHEN SHE LEAVES HERE SHE CAN'T TAKE OUR ELECTRIC WHEELCHAIR WITH HER.

SHE WON'T BE ABLE TO GET ROUND HALF AS WELL WITH A MANUAL WHEELCHAIR. AND, OF COURSE, HER GRAN COULDN'T AFFORD TO BUY AN ELECTRIC ONE.

OH, WHAT A SHAME!

Laura told her friends Alice's story —

COULDN'T WE DO SOMETHING TO HELP HER?

I KNOW! OUR SCHOOL CHARITY FUND-RAISING. EVERY YEAR, IT GOES TO A DIFFERENT CAUSE, RIGHT? WELL, IF YOU THREE GO TO GRIM GERTIE . . .

And —

SO WE WONDERED IF THIS YEAR, THE MONEY COULD GO TO BUY AN ELECTRIC CHAIR FOR ALICE.

I THINK THAT SOUNDS LIKE AN EXCELLENT IDEA, BECKY. I'LL MAKE ENQUIRIES AS TO WHAT IT WOULD COST.

Soon —

I'M SORRY, GIRLS, BUT WE DON'T HAVE QUITE ENOUGH. WE WOULD NEED ANOTHER FIVE HUNDRED POUNDS!

WE COULD RAISE IT!

THERE'S NEARLY A WEEK OF SCHOOL LEFT! COULD WE DO SOME FUND-RAISING, MISS GRIMSTYLE?

Grim Gertie agreed.

SO FOR THE ALICE'S CHAIR FUND, WE'VE AGREED TO DO AN END OF TERM CONCERT. ANY OF YOU WHO CAN DO AN ACT, SING, DANCE, PLAY AN INSTRUMENT, ANYTHING — SEE ME AFTER ASSEMBLY!

I'LL SING FOR YOU. MY MUM SAYS WE SHOULD SUPPORT WORTHY CAUSES.

I CAN TAP DANCE.

EXCELLENT!

FREDDY AND I HAVE OUR OWN BAND. WE DON'T MIND DOING A FEW NUMBERS FOR YOU.

THAT'LL BE A LAUGH! LISTEN, BECKY, WHY DON'T WE DO HALF-TIME REFRESHMENTS? SELL CAKES AND DRINKS.

NICE IDEA, CLAIRE.

At rehearsals —

WE MIGHT MAKE SOME MONEY SELLING EAR PLUGS WITH THESE TWO!

At Laura's —

HODGE AND FREDDY CAN'T KEEP IN TIME, THE DANCE TROUPE HAVE THREE LEFT FEET EACH — I'LL BE MENTAL BY FRIDAY, LAURA!

WISH I COULD BE THERE TO HELP, BECKY, BUT THE DOC SAID I HAVE TO REST. SAVE ME A TICKET, THOUGH — I WOULDN'T MISS THE SHOW FOR ANYTHING!

Next day —

HOW ARE THE TICKETS GOING, NIKKI?

BRILLIANT! EVEN AT A POUND EACH, I'VE NEARLY SOLD OUT!

OH, HELP! LET'S HOPE THE CONCERT GOES OFF ALL RIGHT OR THEY'LL ALL BE WANTING THEIR MONEY BACK.

But, on the night —

IT'S ALL WORKING! MY-MUM-SAYS MARGARET REALLY HAS A LOVELY VOICE.

THE SHOW'S BRILL! I DON'T KNOW WHAT BECKY WAS WORRYING ABOUT!

At the end —

VERY WELL DONE INDEED, EVERYBODY — AND SPECIAL CONGRATULATIONS TO THE PRODUCER, BECKY SINDEN. I AM PLEASED TO TELL YOU, WE HAVE RAISED THE GRAND SUM OF . . .

. . . FIVE HUNDRED AND TWO POUNDS, FORTY-FIVE PENCE!

WE'VE DONE IT!

YAAYY!

Soon —

FOR ME? FOR KEEPS?

TO THINK YOU DID ALL THIS — HOW CAN WE EVER THANK YOU?

I THINK WE CAN INVITE THEM ALL TO OUR CHRISTMAS PARTY, DON'T YOU?

And so —

THANK YOU SO MUCH, MISS GRIMSTYLE.

OUR PLEASURE. I CANNOT THINK OF A BETTER USE FOR REDVALE'S COLLECTION.

SOMETHING REALLY GOOD CAME OF MY BUS ACCIDENT, AFTER ALL. IT REALLY IS A MERRY CHRISTMAS!

THE END

Secret Schoolgirl

CONTINUED FROM PAGE 74

OH!

HELLO! I'M THE SECRETARY'S ASSISTANT. ARE YOU FINDING YOUR WAY ROUND?

WORRIED that someone would find her bag in the dorm, Amy made her way there, disguising herself with some props and a costume from the drama store.

A few minutes later —

ER — YES. EVERYTHING'S FINE.

GOOD! I'LL LEAVE YOU TO IT THEN. DON'T BE AFRAID TO ASK IF THERE ARE ANY PROBLEMS.

POOR GIRL. I BET SHE'S REALLY NERVOUS, STARTING AT A NEW SCHOOL.

Later—

I WANTED TO BUY SOME CHOCOLATE BISCUITS FOR YOU, AMY, BUT I'VE LOST MY POCKET MONEY. SORRY!

DON'T WORRY, NINA. I'VE PLENTY HERE.

WE'D BETTER GO NOW. THAT NEW GIRL, SANDRA, KEEPS HANGING AROUND AND WE DON'T WANT HER TO KNOW WHAT'S GOING ON.

HA! CAUGHT YOU! COME ON — WHAT ARE YOU HIDING IN THERE? LET ME SEE!

OH! IT'S — ER — NOTHING, BRENDA. WE'RE JUST HAVING A GAME.

GET OUT OF MY WAY! I'LL FIND OUT WHAT'S GOING ON.

HONESTLY, BRENDA — IT'S NOTHING.

HUH! THERE'S NOTHING HERE. YOU'RE JUST TRYING TO MAKE A FOOL OF ME. WELL — YOU CAN BOTH TAKE A DETENTION FOR CHEEKING A PREFECT!

PHEW! THAT WAS CLOSE. BUT WHERE'S AMY? SHE'S VANISHED!

Later, when Brenda had gone—

AMY! WHERE ARE YOU?

THAT FOOLED YOU! I HEARD BRENDA TALKING TO YOU OUTSIDE, SO I DIVED INTO THE BASKET.

BRILL! YOU HAD US REALLY WORRIED — WE THOUGHT YOU'D DISAPPEARED!

LOOK — PERHAPS I'D BETTER GO. SOMEONE'S BOUND TO FIND OUT ABOUT ME SOONER OR LATER AND THEN YOU'LL ALL BE IN TROUBLE.

BUT, AMY! YOU'VE NOWHERE TO GO TO. DON'T WORRY ABOUT IT — IT'S GREAT HAVING YOU HERE AS A SECRET SCHOOLGIRL! WE'LL LOOK AFTER YOU!

Later—

IT'S NO GOOD. I CAN'T STAY HERE. IT'S NOT FAIR TO THE OTHERS. THEY'VE BEEN GREAT, HELPING ME OUT LIKE THIS, BUT WHEN THE SECRET'S OUT THEY COULD BE EXPELLED.

I'LL LEAVE A NOTE HERE FOR JANE. SHE'LL FIND IT THIS AFTERNOON WHEN SHE CHANGES FOR THE HOCKEY PRACTICE. OH — SOMEONE'S COMING! I'D BETTER HIDE!

IT'S SANDRA, THE NEW GIRL! WHAT'S SHE DOING?

SHE'S STEALING FROM THE LOCKERS. I REMEMBER NOW, SHE WAS LOOKING IN NINA'S WARDROBE WHEN I SAW HER IN THE DORMITORY — SHE MUST HAVE TAKEN NINA'S POCKET MONEY.

BANG!

WHO'S THAT?

As Sandra panicked, she ran straight into a teacher —

WHAT'S GOING ON? YOU SHOULDN'T BE IN HERE. WHY — WHAT'S ALL THIS?

I THINK YOU HAVE SOME EXPLAINING TO DO, YOUNG LADY.

I'D BETTER GO. THE POLICE MAY BE CALLED AND I DON'T WANT TO BE FOUND HERE.

But, before Amy could escape—

DON'T WORRY, MISS LENNOX — WE'LL DEAL WITH THIS. BY THE WAY, HAVE YOU HAD ANY NEWS OF AMY HOWARD? WE'RE STILL LOOKING FOR HER. THERE WAS A CHANCE SHE MIGHT COME BACK HERE, WASN'T THERE?

SO THEY ARE LOOKING FOR ME! AUNTIE BETTY MUST HAVE REPORTED ME MISSING. I'LL HAVE TO GET AWAY — I JUST CAN'T BEAR THE THOUGHT OF GOING BACK TO HER.

But as Amy ran —

AAGH!

Amy was knocked unconscious—

WHY — THERE'S ONE OF THE GIRLS, AND IT LOOKS LIKE SHE'S HURT. I'D BETTER GET HELP.

Some time later, when Amy came round—

MUM! DAD! IT CAN'T BE! I THOUGHT YOU WERE BOTH DEAD!

BY A MIRACLE WE SURVIVED THE AIR CRASH AND WERE FOUND BY THE RESCUERS. IT'S *YOU* WE'VE BEEN WORRYING ABOUT! THE POLICE WERE LOOKING FOR YOU TO TELL YOU WE WERE SAFE, BUT NO-ONE KNEW WHERE YOU'D GONE.

OH, I CAN'T BELIEVE YOU'RE REALLY HERE. NOW EVERYTHING WILL BE ALL RIGHT!

NO-ONE NEEDS TO KNOW I WAS HIDING IN THE SCHOOL. THAT'S OUR SECRET.

So, a few days later—

WELCOME BACK, AMY!

THERE'S NO NEED TO HIDE YOU NOW! IT'LL BE LIKE OLD TIMES!

IT'S GREAT TO BE BACK!

THE NIGHTMARE'S OVER NOW. I'M BACK AT SCHOOL WITH MY FRIENDS. I DON'T HAVE TO BE A SECRET SCHOOLGIRL ANY MORE!

THE END

104

107

The End

IT'S NICE TO SEE YOU LOOKING SO SMART, FRAN. DON'T YOU FEEL GOOD?

ER — YES — OF COURSE.

HUH! NOT LIKELY! BUT IF THINGS WORK OUT, I'LL GET OUT OF WEARING IT THIS AFTERNOON!

Soon —

HAPPY BIRTHDAY, GRAN!

THANKS, LOVE! HOW NICE TO SEE YOU. MY WORD, FRAN! YOU DO LOOK SMART TODAY!

Then —

HI, SANDY! CAN I TAKE SANDY FOR A RUN, GRAN?

OF COURSE. BE CAREFUL NOT TO SPOIL YOUR NEW DRESS!

DON'T WORRY, GRAN. I CAME PREPARED!

FRAN! YOU'VE CHANGED! WHAT ARE YOU DOING?

JUST TAKING SANDY OUT FOR A WALK. I HAD TO CHANGE SO I WOULDN'T MESS UP MY NEW DRESS.

A few days later, the school holidays began.

CAN I HAVE A LIFT ON THURSDAY AFTERNOON, MUM? I'M MEETING SHARON AT THE POOL AT FOUR O'CLOCK.

WELL, I'VE ARRANGED A PHOTO SESSION FOR SOME OF MY DESIGNS ON THURSDAY AFTERNOON, BUT WE SHOULD BE FINISHED BY HALF-PAST THREE. IF YOU COME WITH ME, I COULD DROP YOU OFF AT THE POOL AFTERWARDS. HOW'S THAT?

THAT'S FINE. THANKS, MUM.

IT'LL BE A MEGA-BORING SESSION, BUT I SUPPOSE I'LL HAVE TO SIT THROUGH IT IF I WANT A LIFT.

On Thursday —

HELLO, ANNABEL. WHO'S THIS YOU'VE BROUGHT WITH YOU?

HI, STEVE. THIS IS MY DAUGHTER, FRAN. SHE'S COME TO WATCH.

YOU COULD BE JUST WHAT I'M LOOKING FOR, FRAN! I'VE BEEN ASKED TO PHOTOGRAPH A NEW RANGE OF TEENAGE CLOTHES AND YOU'D BE JUST RIGHT! HOW ABOUT IT?

OH! WELL — ER — I DON'T KNOW.

NO WAY! I BET THEY'LL BE SOPPY DRESSES AND STUPID SHOES!

OF COURSE SHE'LL DO IT! WON'T YOU, LOVE?

WELL — I — OH, ALL RIGHT.

LOOKS LIKE I'VE NO CHOICE!

THAT'S GREAT! COME ROUND HERE ON SATURDAY. WE SHOULD GET IT DONE IN A MORNING.

HELP! WHAT HAVE I LET MYSELF IN FOR?

But, on Saturday —

IT'S SUCH A PITY THIS FASHION CONFERENCE HAS CROPPED UP TODAY. I'D LOVE TO HAVE WATCHED YOUR FIRST FASHION SHOOT, FRAN!

NEVER MIND, MUM!

IT'LL BE BAD ENOUGH WITHOUT MUM THERE FUSSING AROUND!

111

TAKE SOME SHOES AND BELTS OF YOUR OWN TO WEAR WITH THE DIFFERENT OUTFITS — AND THESE BAGS AND SCARVES. YOU MIGHT NEED THEM.

OKAY.

OH, NO! I WISH I'D NEVER SAID I'D DO THIS.

Later —

HAVE A LOOK AROUND IN THERE, THEN WE'LL DO SOME SHOTS IN HERE BEFORE HEADING OUT TO THE PARK.

I'LL NEVER LIVE IT DOWN IF ANY OF MY MATES SEE ME IN THE PARK IN A LOAD OF FANCY CLOTHES. I WISH I'D NEVER COME!

Back home —

HOW DID IT GO, FRAN? I JUST CAN'T BELIEVE IT — MY SCRUFFY LITTLE TOMBOY BEING A MODEL!

IT WENT OKAY, BUT YOU'LL HAVE TO WAIT UNTIL THE MAG COMES OUT TO SEE THE PICTURES.

A few weeks later —

THERE! WHAT DO YOU THINK, MUM?

OH! BUT — ER — THAT'S WHAT YOU USUALLY LOOK LIKE!

I KNOW! IT WAS A NEW RANGE OF JEANS AND TOPS STEVE WAS PHOTOGRAPHING, SO I DIDN'T MIND AT ALL. I REALLY ENJOYED IT!

NO WONDER YOU WOULDN'T TELL ME ABOUT IT!

YOU WIN, FRAN! YOU LOOK REALLY GOOD IN THOSE PHOTOS, SO THAT MUST BE YOUR STYLE. I RECKON I'LL NEVER CHANGE YOU, HOWEVER MUCH I TRY!

THANKS, MUM! MAYBE ONE DAY I'LL WEAR FRILLY DRESSES, BUT FOR THE MOMENT, I'LL STICK WITH MY JEANS!

THE END

Presenting Christmas

Here's how to make those crimbo pressies look extra special. It's easy!

114

Top Tips
★ Fold the edges of the paper over before you stick them down for neat corners.

★ Pack fragile gifts in plenty of tissue paper so they survive the Christmas morning scramble.

★ Save ribbons and bows during the year and recycle by using them for your Christmas pressies.

Big Bow
This big bow is just 12 equal lengths of ribbon made into loops. Ours is lick 'n' stick ribbon to make it easy. Place the loops on top of each other at angles and secure with a staple through the middle.

★ All our ribbon and paper came from a selection available at Hallmark card shops!

Party Present
This is an ideal party gift — it comes with balloons and party footer attached. We used ribbon to tie them on.

★ Make excellent gift tags by cutting out designs on the front of last year's crimbo cards, making a hole with a paper punch and threading through some ribbon.

Bow Now!
Make this big bow by folding a piece of tissue paper in two and then making a fan by folding on either side and tying in the centre with ribbon. One big bow's nice, but you could make lots of little ones too!

Snow Row
This row of snowmen was made by cutting out the design from some left-over paper. We threaded them together to make an ace gift tag.

Santa's Sack
We made this clever Santa sack by wrapping a piece of paper round a video tape! Just wrap the bottom end as you would a normal present and then slide the video out of the other end. Your sack's made! Staple or glue on handles made from ribbon or string. The paper stuffing is ideal for hiding a selection of small gifts. To make — fold up a piece of tissue paper and cut lengths off, then unravel them and use to fill your sack.

Do The Twist
Cut the top of a circular present into strands and then twist to make a pineapple effect. Add a bow or two if you like!

Christmas Cracker
A bottle or awkward shaped gift can be made into this wicked cracker. Twist the ends and tie with ribbon (we used some left-over lace — but you could use a paper doily). Some bows finish it off.

Sweet Thing
These wrapped sweeties make a pretty decoration — and they're a tasty treat too! Just tie the ends of them together and stick on or tie with ribbon.

Penny Pressies
Chocolate pennies stuck on to ribbon or paper packages look pretty. Use double-sided sticky tape or loops of normal sellotape to secure them.

Curly Wurly!
Curling ribbon looks ace! Just run the blade of your scissors along the length of the ribbon to make lovely spirals. We also made this gift tag by cutting out a tree design from wrapping paper and sticking it on to card.

THE RIGHT TIME

IT was Saturday afternoon and thirteen-year-old Rachel Thomas was busy tidying her room —

HI, RACHEL! YOUR MUM SENT US UP. GOSH, YOU'VE BEEN TIDYING. YOUR ROOM LOOKS NEAT.

THANKS, SUE. IT WAS CERTAINLY NEEDING IT! WHAT ARE YOU TWO UP TO?

I GAVE MY TEDDY AWAY WHEN I WAS EIGHT. MIND YOU, HE WAS A BIT THREADBARE. YOURS IS IN GOOD CONDITION.

WE'RE GOING TO THE FAIR ON THE COMMON. DAD GAVE ME SOME EXTRA MONEY. WANT TO COME?

I'LL JUST PUT TED BACK IN HIS USUAL PLACE.

I TAKE CARE OF TED — HE BELONGED TO MY GREAT-GRANDMOTHER.

GO ON, RACHEL. IT'LL BE FUN.

OH, OKAY THEN.

YOU AND YOUR TEDDY! YOU'RE TOO OLD TO HAVE HIM, REALLY!

BUT I STILL LOVE HIM.

I HAVEN'T GOT AS MUCH MONEY AS SUE AND BECKY. MY DAD'S BEEN OUT OF WORK.

COME ON, YOU TWO! WE'RE MISSING THE FAIR!

115

'BYE, LOVE. HAVE A GOOD TIME.

MUM LOOKS SAD. DAD HAD ANOTHER REFUSAL FOR A JOB THIS MORNING.

On the common —

LOOK, BECKY! THERE'S A FRIEND OF RACHEL'S! HA! HA!

THEY'RE ALWAYS TEASING ME ABOUT TED, BUT I DON'T MIND.

Soon —

OH, NO — A THUNDERSTORM! WE'VE NO COATS — WE'D BETTER GET HOME!

Back home —

MUM, DO YOU THINK I'M TOO OLD TO STILL HAVE MY TEDDY? DO YOU THINK I SHOULD GIVE HIM AWAY?

NOT IF YOU DON'T WANT TO, LOVE. GIVE HIM AWAY WHEN YOU'RE READY TO. YOU'LL KNOW WHEN THE TIME IS RIGHT.

HOW WILL I KNOW, MUM?

YOU'LL KNOW. IT WILL JUST FEEL RIGHT.

Later —

THESE EXPERTS KNOW SO MUCH ABOUT ANTIQUES. FANCY THAT VASE BEING WORTH £10,000!

IT'S HORRIBLE! I WOULDN'T HAVE IT IN THE HOUSE!

SO THAT'S ALL FROM THE ANTIQUES SHOW FOR THIS WEEK. NEXT WEEK WE'LL BE IN ROSSFORD . . .

THEY'RE COMING HERE! HOW EXCITING!

SHALL WE GO AND HAVE DAD VALUED THEN, MUM? HA! HA!

Next day, at school —

MY GRAN'S GOING TO TAKE A PAINTING, TO SEE HOW MUCH IT'S WORTH.

EVERYBODY'S EXCITED ABOUT THE ANTIQUES SHOW COMING TO ROSSFORD.

LET'S ALL GO AND WATCH. WE MIGHT EVEN GET ON TELLY!

YES, LET'S. THEY SHOW THE PROGRAMME LATER, SO WE'LL BE ABLE TO SEE OURSELVES!

So, the following week —

GOSH, IT'S CROWDED! OH, LOOK AT THAT UGLY VASE!

BET IT'S WORTH A BOMB!

ANTIQUE ROAD SHOW

JUST LOOK AT THAT GIRL. SHE MUST BE ABOUT FIFTEEN AND SHE'S BROUGHT HER DOLLY WITH HER!

MAYBE SHE'S GOT A TEDDY BEAR AS WELL, LIKE RACHEL!

SHUT UP, YOU TWO! THERE'S NOTHING WRONG WITH MY TED, ALTHOUGH I DON'T THINK I'D BE BRAVE ENOUGH TO CARRY IT OUTSIDE.

Soon —

IF YOU WERE TO TAKE THIS TABLE TO AUCTION, IT WOULD PROBABLY SELL FOR AROUND £3,000.

WOW! AND SHE SAID IT'S BEEN IN HER ATTIC FOR YEARS.

Then —

OH, THAT GIRL'S GOING TO HAVE HER DOLL VALUED.

WHAT A LOVELY VICTORIAN CHINA DOLL!

THERE'S SOME SLIGHT DAMAGE HERE, BUT OTHERWISE IT'S IN EXCELLENT CONDITION. AT AUCTION THIS DOLL SHOULD FETCH £2,500. ARE YOU GOING TO SELL HER?

OH, NO. SHE'S A FAMILY HEIRLOOM.

However, Sue's gran's painting was a fake —

FAKE OR NOT — I STILL LIKE IT!

POOR MRS MILLAR — STILL, SHE DOESN'T SEEM TOO DISAPPOINTED.

Later, back home —

THE GUIDES ARE HAVING A SALE NEXT WEEK IN AID OF FAMINE RELIEF. I TOLD THEM YOU'D SORT OUT SOME OLD BOOKS AND THINGS.

OKAY, MUM, I'LL DO IT NOW.

So —

I'VE GOT LOADS OF STUFF ALREADY. MAYBE THIS IS THE TIME TO GIVE UP TED?

NO, I'LL KEEP HIM. THEY WOULDN'T GET MUCH MONEY FOR OLD TED ANYWAY.

The following week —

WE'LL HAVE TO CUT DOWN ON THAT, THEN, AND SEE IF WE CAN SPEND LESS ON HEATING.

MUM AND DAD WORRY ABOUT MONEY ALL THE TIME. POOR DAD CAN'T GET A JOB ANYWHERE!

That afternoon —

LOOK, THERE'S RACHEL ON TV!

AND SUE AND BECKY!

THERE ARE SOME LOVELY THINGS, AREN'T THERE?

THERE'S GOING TO BE AN AUCTION IN TOWN NEXT WEEK. PEOPLE CAN TAKE THE ITEMS THEY'VE JUST SHOWN AND ANYTHING ELSE AS WELL.

WELL, I'M OFF TO THE GUIDES SALE NOW. I SAID I'D MEET SUE AND BECKY THERE. I'LL JUST PUT TED UPSTAIRS.

THERE YOU ARE, TED. I WON'T BE LONG.

Soon —

HEY, THIS IS ALL ABOUT OLD POP STARS. LET'S HAVE A LOOK.

MM, "OLD TOYS AND DOLLS".

THESE PICTURES ARE LOVELY.

LOOK AT THAT HAIRSTYLE! HA! HA!

FANCY THERE BEING A GROUP CALLED DAVE DEE, DOZY, BEAKY, MICK AND TITCH!

OH, THIS IS INTERESTING.

Old Toys AND Dolls

On the way home —

HM, I WONDER . . .

WHAT'S UP WITH RACHEL? SHE'S IN A WORLD OF HER OWN.

A few days later —

YOU KNOW THE ANTIQUES AUCTION YOU WERE TALKING ABOUT, DAD? IT'S ON THIS EVENING. CAN WE GO AND WATCH?

GOOD IDEA, RACHEL. YES, WE'LL ALL GO.

So —

WE'LL NOT BE BUYING ANYTHING, THOUGH, THAT'S FOR SURE.

Soon —

OOH, DOESN'T HE TALK FAST?

WHATEVER YOU DO, DON'T NOD OR SHAKE YOUR HEAD! HE'LL THINK WE'RE BIDDING!

LOOK WHAT THEY'RE AUCTIONING NEXT! A TEDDY BEAR!

NEXT WE HAVE A GERMAN-MADE TEDDY BEAR. A VERY GOOD EXAMPLE OF THIS PARTICULAR MODEL. WHO WILL START THE BIDDING AT £500?

£500?

£1,000 . . . £1,500 . . . £2,000 . . .

IT'S AMAZING! A LOT OF PEOPLE SEEM TO WANT IT! IT MUST BE REALLY VALUABLE!

Finally —

SOLD AT £3,200 TO THE LADY ON THE RIGHT!

WHAT A PRICE! AND IT DOESN'T LOOK ANY DIFFERENT FROM RACHEL'S TEDDY!

Soon —

YOU GO WITHOUT ME. I'LL CATCH YOU UP LATER.

ALL RIGHT THEN, LOVE. DON'T BE LATE.

And, when Rachel arrived home —

MUM! DAD! I'VE GOT GREAT NEWS! THAT TEDDY AT THE AUCTION *WAS* MINE! HERE'S THE CHEQUE — I WANT YOU TO HAVE IT!

THIS IS WONDERFUL! BUT HOW DID YOU KNOW TED WAS VALUABLE?

I READ A BOOK AT THE GUIDE SALE ABOUT VALUABLE TOYS — THERE WAS A PICTURE OF TED IN IT!

OH, RACHEL! FANCY YOUR TEDDY BEING WORTH SO MUCH! BUT YOU DIDN'T *HAVE* TO SELL HIM. WE KNOW YOU LOVED HIM.

THE TIME WAS RIGHT, MUM. THE TIME WAS RIGHT.

The End

BUNTY— A girl like you

Starring YOU!

SPECIAL £10 WINNERS

We called up these Bunty readers to find out all about them. Which one supports Rangers football team and which one wants to be a model? Read on and find out!

★ ★ ★

Here's Katie McCormack from West Lothian pictured at EuroDisney on her hols. In the McCormack family there's Mum and Dad, Margaret and Tom and sister, Sarah. Also Flora the dog, Ben the cat and Jockey the budgie!

STAR FILE

- **fave Bunty story** — Luv, Lisa
- **likes** — horse-riding
- **fave food** — pizza and chips
- **ambition** — to be a nurse
- **fave popsters** — Take That
- **mega-bores** — school and tidying up
- **TV faves** — Home and Away and Children's Ward
- **fact** — she plays piano and cornet
- **best friend** — Hayley
- **Troll collection** — 12
- **wants to meet** — actress Melissa Bell or Michael Jackson
- **3 wishes** — to own her own horse, to go to Florida, to meet Rangers Football team

Katie goes cartoon crazy at EuroDisney

All dressed up!

Lynsey McKernan is from Co. Armagh. She's got two brothers — Leon and Ross. Mum and Dad are Rosemary and Seamus.

STAR FILE

- **likes** — rollerskating, cycling, drawing, dancing, horses
- **plays** — trombone
- **pen pals** — Louise from Liverpool and Lyndsay from Cheshire
- **fave dinner** — corn on the cob, sausage and chips and pavlova!
- **mega-bores** — stew and spiders
- **pop faves** — ABBA and Take That
- **Bunty fave** — The Four Marys
- **wants to meet** — Take That
- **film faves** — Beetlejuice, Problem Child 1 & 2, Sister Act and Bill and Ted
- **ambitions** — to be a model or an art teacher
- **collections** — soaps, badges, keyrings, Buntys
- **best mates** — Mary and Shauna
- **fact** — she goes to speech and drama and Girl Guides
- **3 wishes** — to be a Bunty cover girl, to go to Jamaica on holiday, to have an American accent!

Suzanne's a star!

Meet Suzanne Stokes from London. She has two brothers — Andrew and Jonathan. Then there's Clover, her pet rabbit.

STAR FILE

- **likes** — swimming, school, netball and spending money!
- **fave day** — Friday when her Bunty arrives
- **plays** — recorder
- **TV faves** — Family Ties, Full House and the Discovery Channel all on cable TV
- **mega-bores** — fish for dinner and spiders in her bedroom
- **wants to meet** — Mark Owen from Take That
- **Bunty fave** — Luv, Lisa
- **collections** — Trolls, Sylvanian Families, stamps
- **ambitions** — to be an archaeologist and study dinosaurs
- **best friends** — Amanda and Alice
- **fave food** — pizza
- **fact** — she collects money for charities — especially the NSPCC
- **3 wishes** — to be famous
  to win a million pounds
  to go to DisneyWorld

Brothers Andrew and Jonathan get in on the act!

Bonnie bunny!

What a poser!

...nsey and her trombone!

Dionne with best mate, Gemma, on a school trip

Dionne Lorraine Moffat is from Washington in Tyne and Wear. The Moffats include Mum and Dad — Sonia and Geoff, brother, Gary who wants to be a rock star and big sis, Karen. Then there's Glen the dog, Thumper the rabbit and a whole tankful of tropical fish!

STAR FILE

- **likes** — reading Bunty
- **pop faves** — Madonna, Cher, N.K.O.T.B.
- **ambition** — to be famous
- **wants** — to be a model
- **fave film** — Drop Dead Fred
- **mega-bores** — getting up in the morning and being untidy
- **TV faves** — Home and Away and Neighbours
- **loves** — dancing
- **collects** — rubbers
- **fact** — she plays the viola
- **wants to meet** — Madonna
- **fave Bunty story** — The Four Marys
- **best mates** — sister, Karen, Gemma, Michelle, Donna, Laura, Kelly
- **3 wishes** — to be rich
  to own a pony
  to go to Florida

Dionne goes for a quiet swim on holiday in Cyprus